LET US THINK AND TALK NIGERIA FIRST

C. ANGUSLAZ ANOKWUTE

Ask not what your country will do for you, but ask what you will do for your country.

— John F. Kennedy, former U.S. President

I will not be interested in politics if it does not concern the people; if it doesn't concern men and women like myself. It doesn't make any sense to me.

— Prof. Yemi Osinbajo.

A **National Patriotism** Publication.

NIGERIA PLEDGE

I pledge to Nigeria my country
To be faithful, loyal and honest
To serve Nigeria with all my strength
To defend her unity and uphold her honor and glory
So help me God.

NIGERIA ANTHEM

Arise, O compatriots,
Nigeria's call obey
To serve our fatherland
With love and strength and faith,
The labour of our heroes past
Shall never be in vain
To serve with heart and might
One nation bound in freedom
Peace and unity,

Oh God of creation
Direct our noble cause,
Guide our leaders right
Help our youths the truth to know
In love and honesty to grow
And living just and true
Great lofty heights attain,
To build a nation where peace
And justice shall reign.

DEDICATION

To the President of Nigeria,
To every one good in the Executive, in the Legislature,
in the Judiciary— at all the levels of government:
worthy leaders who seriously
and tirelessly work for Nigeria to work.

To our founding Fathers –
Zik, Awo, Belewa, etal, patriotic:
selfless leaders who fought for One Nigeria –
with the vision of an egalitarian and just society
where peace and unity shall reign.

PREFACE

There is a saying in Igbo that those who do not know where the rain started beating them will not know where it will stop beating them. It surely gives no joy telling the past of Nigeria, because Nigerian history represents gory tales of atrocities and matchless aberrations—events quite inciting. But at the same time, we ignore this same history at our own peril as the famous American Historian, Santayana, observed. The knowledge of the past gives room for correction in the future. It is a popular saying that united we stand, and divided we fall. But my country seems to disobey this time-acknowledged logic. In this light, therefore, Nigeria seems to me an irony, a perplexing paradox. This is so because our unity has left sour taste in the mouths of many, if not all, of the constituent tribes in this entity: to the extent that at the last count, none willingly stands for Nigeria but for own tribe, region or religion. Hence, Nigeria remains an orphan, or at best the proverbial goat owned by many people which dies of hunger. Everything is evaluated on the scale of tribalism or alliance to some religion.

Most of our leaders are chameleons that are neither here nor there on national issues when their opinions matter most. These disgruntled elements always incite their people against others when things never favoured them. And most times, this stance dovetails into undue tensions in the polity. I dare say that most riots in the country could have not occurred in the first place, if not for the selfish influences of heartless leaders we have. Surely, leadership has frontally failed Nigerians for quite a long time now.

Another disturbing index in the life of the Nigerian state is the twin monster of bribery and corruption. In any case, the government of the day is still battling with this monster of bribery and corruption. And this, surely, is a war that must be won. Nigeria's image, everyone knows, has been a very bad one, so battered into shame by both aliens and Nigerians themselves. Surely, we have to, indeed, acknowledge that some Nigerians are corrupt, and that there are so many ills in the land as it is in other countries of the world. But we must also appreciate the fact that it is not all bad about this country.

Whatever is the case or image, the truth is that at the centre of Nigeria's woes (real or imagined) is lack of patriotism. It is lack of love for one's country that will make someone to shamelessly loot public funds, vandalize national assets, collect and give bribe, refuse to report criminal activities to law enforcement agents, refuse to contribute to nation-building, but rather indulge in unwholesome habits or sharp practices. The activities of those infinitesimally few number of unpatriotic elements have since made the ship of the nation drift off-course against the visions of the Founding Fathers of the Nigerian nation, whilst the Nigerian project has seemingly assumed the status of a lame duck. But those of us in majority, we see hope for Nigeria, we see a re-branded Nigeria that will once more stand proudly tall among the comity of nations, to command the full respect she deserves.

It is my opinion that we all as citizens need proper (re-)orientation, whilst Nigeria as a country needs re-branding. We must imbibe the culture of thinking Nigeria in all things, we must use our talents (and whatever resources available to us) to contribute to nation-building, for we have no other place to call our own

This poetical piece of patriotism is targeted at instilling national-consciousness in the citizenry, with the ultimate aim of sparking-up the light of nationalism or patriotism in our people— old and young. It is an attempt at lending my patriotic voice in times like this— thinking and talking Nigeria first, whilst inspiring generations of our people.

Engr. C. AnguslazAnokwute

Abuja, Nigeria
1 January, 2014.

CONTENTS

PART 1

X-RAYING THE VISIONS OF OUR FOUDING FATHERS

ONE NIGERIA

That I should be an instrument of power
To tower high above my countrymen
And hold their rein at our momentous hour,
Was offering made in an Onitsha den
Had East and West united to divide
The spoils of war whilst caring not a fig,
Our vaunted unity would be descried,
The freedom we had won would then renege.
"The South is smaller than the North, my friends,
Can we afford to rend our unity
Because we wish to serve our private ends,
Rather than keep intact our entity?"
To be or not to be, confronted me:
I made my choice, by shunning infamy.

—Rt. Hon. Dr. Nnamdi Azikiwe.

It is important that ill-will be not created. The North and the South are one.

—Dr Nnamdi Azikiwe.

As a young man I saw visions: visions of Nigeria becoming a great country in the emerging continent of Africa; visions of Nigeria offering freedom to those in bondage, and securing the democratic way of life to those who had been lulled into an illusion of security under colonial rule... I trust that I shall dream my dreams amid the peace and ever increasing prosperity of the people of my native Nigeria. The motto of the independent federation of Nigeria is Unity and Faith. I pray that we may guard our unity and keep our faith. I fought against British rule, because I honestly believed that it denied me and my people the basic freedoms and fundamental rights. At the material time, I believed, as I still do, that in normal times no man should impose his rule on any people unless he has been elected to do so at a free and fair election. It was an article of faith with me that an African citizen should enjoy individual freedom under the law.

–Dr Nnamdi Azikiwe.

Let me take this opportunity to warn those who are making a mountain out of the molehill of..crisis to be more restrained and constructive. The dissemination of lies abroad; the publishing of flamboyant headlines about secessionist plans, and the goading of empty-headed careerists with gaseous ideas about their own importance in tile scheme of things .. is being overdone in certain quarters. I feel that these quarters must be held responsible for any breach between the North and South, which nature had indissolubly united in a political, social and economic marriage of convenience. In my personal opinion, there is no sense in the North breaking away or the East or the West breaking away; it would be better if all the regions would address themselves to the task of crystallizing common nationality, irrespective of the extraneous influences at work. What history has joined together let no man put asunder.

–Dr Nnamdi Azikiwe, 1953.

The nationalists fought for independence. They were on the radical or revolutionary side of independence. There was evolutionary side of it. But the important thing is that Sardauna's NPC and Awolowo's Action Group and Azikiwe's NCNC agreed to work together in the struggle for independence. They jointly demanded independence from Britain..we envisaged and planned for a great country in Africa, a country that would give leadership, moral leadership, economic leadership, and political leadership to the rest of Africa. But unfortunately, the nationalists were only empowered and in control for six months, when the most unpatriotic military turned the arms the nationalist gave to them to protect and defend the country, on the nationalists...and remained in power for about thirty something years. The military stayed in power, thereby destroying values, destroying political history of the country. They don't want the history of the country to be known.

—Mbazuluike Amaechi, Nationalist.

-

Although I was young in 1960, I knew that Azikiwe always called on Akintola, Awolowo, Ahmadu Bello, Okpara and others to join him to build a new Nigeria.

—Kalu Idika Kalu.

PART 2

NIGERIA VEERING OFF COURSE INTO SOBSTORY:

Those who do not learn from history are doomed to repeat it.
- George Santayana (American Poet and Historian).

No, I don't love my country if pointing out what is unjust in what we love amounts to not loving, if insisting that what we love should measure up to the finest image we have of her amounts to not loving.

- Albert Camus.

We have in our midst .. rich Nigerians who in the past cleverly rigged the sources of the wealth of our nation, and we are now tactically poised to oligopolise all the munificent avenues of riches that may supervene now and in the future. The rich, and the highly-placed in business, public life, and government, are running a dreadful risk in their callous neglect of the poor and down-trodden.

–Obafemi Awolowo.

Fantastic. Life in Nigeria before independence was interesting. It was peaceful. It was progressive and constructive. It was anything but bad. Even immediately after independence, up to 1965, everything in Nigeria was orderly. There was discipline; there was decency; there was respect for the elders and people were godly. People were industrious and hard working. People were living positive lives. People were struggling constructively to become something in life. Nothing was cheap and nothing was taken for granted. We made a lot of progress between 1950 and 1960. Life was fantastic. I cannot compare life at the time to anything today…Our economy was actually developing fast, we had cocoa..in the then Western Region…The economy was buoyant. That was because it was agro-based economy…We were all very busy and in those days we were exporting a lot of things. So, the economy was a lot better.
The Nigerian pound was equal to the British pound. The banking industry was just developing at the time.

—Chief Alani Bankole.

What kind of country is that? It is a useless country, not the country itself is useless but the people who are running the affairs of the country. They are simply opportunists who do not bother to know the history of the country. They do not bother to know how what they are enjoying now was created, how it was brought about, how the cake they are enjoying now was baked, and the struggle people made to achieve it. What we want is good leadership; give the people good government. But from the military..what do we see? It is massive stealing, massive looting, corruption and destruction of what was created. So, we are celebrating..years of independence but the question is what was achieved in the ..years? I, for example, set up the Ministry Of Aviation; I inherited three pieces of piston engine aircraft only from the West African Airways Corporation. After Ghana and Nigeria became independent they disbanded what was then known as West African Airways Corporation. Then I formed the Nigeria Airways with three aircraft only. At the time I left the ministry, I increased the fleet to 18 aircrafts including 10 intercontinental big body jets. I set up the aviation training school, Zaria, set up instrument landing devices in Kano and Port Harcourt airports. Today all those structures are destroyed. All the places were sold and Nigeria Airways dissolved. Nigeria has no national carrier. But we have some planes owned by some governors who did not own a Peugeot car before they became governors, who now run a fleet of aircraft. That is the nature of corruption and rottenness Nigerian finds itself.

—Mbazuluike Amaechi, Nationalist.

Nigeria was ripe at the time it became independent. What went wrong was when the military assumed power by force. And you know the military is trained for one thing: to destroy, to kill, to massacre and to loot. The military is not trained to manage. It is only when the enemy comes to invade, they try to kill the enemy, destroy the enemy and loot his property. That is what they are trained for. So it was a long interruption of the military in the governance of Nigeria that brought about what we now call the shame of this country. .. there was a time when there was nothing like power failure, where electricity never failed. There was a time in Nigeria when pipe-borne water was running 24 hours. There was a time in Nigeria, when people travelled from Onitsha to Lagos in the night, no armed robbery, no stealing, and no violence. There was a time in Nigeria when workers were paid at the end of the month. And at the end of their career they collect their gratuity on the last day of their work in office and the following month they started collecting their pension. There was this time in Nigeria. And at that time we had no oil. Nigeria had no gas. From 1970, we developed oil well and wealth and the military officers saw that and they were carrying the proceeds to their bank accounts overseas. The military now handed over to politicians who collaborated with them in stealing, who were contractors or their friends and so forth…the military introduced corruption and looting…If Nigerians want the rottenness to continue let them elect them… if Nigerians want to elect such people let them go ahead.

—Mbazuluike Amaechi, Nationalist.

I believe Nigeria..has a lot to celebrate and also, a lot of disappointments to reflect on. We started off at independence with a country like Malaysia, and now Malaysia is so far ahead of us. That is one of the major disappointments. In terms of our social sector, the level of unemployment, particularly youths and graduates unemployment and the state of our infrastructure, we have not done well. These are the major disappointments. Well, the blame is essentially at the door of leadership… it is also an achievement that we have remained one country, unified and we are matching on in unity. And internationally, we had at some points, very high profile. At the moment, we are hitting a low point but I am sure that after the forthcoming elections, which we have been promised will be free, fair and credible, our international profile will rise again.

–Chief Emeka Anyaoku.

Looking back now, we have a lot to thank God for but at the same time, we could have done much better that we did. And we know that not only because we are dissatisfied but because we can compare ourselves with some countries that were at par with us in 1960 and have gone way ahead of us without any oil wealth.

–Archbishop John Onaiyekan.

Well, like our leader said recently, the journey has so far been too bad and it is unfortunate. He gave examples of countries like Malaysia, India, and Saudi Arabia; in fact, countries that we started together in the late 50s and early 60s. They are now all very far ahead of us, and we have more resources than most of these countries. But our wealth is being stolen and it is unfortunate that we have not been awake to our responsibilities.

–Sen. Rufa'i Hanga.

There is abject poverty in the land. The distance between the rich and the poor is too wide… we should try and bridge that gap, so that

Nigerian children can go to school without their parents paying through their noses, so that our senior citizens can get pension at the end of every month without dying of starvation. All Nigerians are asking for is a good leader who is just, fair and passionate about the country and the people. That's all we are asking for.

-Chief Eddie Onuzuruike.

Nigeria has huge population and huge resources yet we are still far behind ..we have not managed our resources to the advantage of our people ... Every Nigerian knows that this country is not developed and so we must determine to develop Nigeria.

-Mallam Adamu Ciroma.

It is not an achievement for Nigerians to acquire money legally and illegally and then go and acquire properties in U. S and Europe...when they know that their own environment is not developed... the painful thing is we know we have the resources and the personnel to be a great nation.

-Mallam Adamu Ciroma.

Corruption is obviously one of the causes for our underdevelopment and we must do something about it... we have to tackle what is it that makes people to be corrupt in Nigeria. Corruption is killing the nation. We all have to accept the responsibility to do the right thing. We must stop paying lip service to the issue of corruption.

-Mallam Adamu Ciroma.

Leadership failed to acknowledge our diversity of resources. What went wrong was that we threw away democratic process. What went wrong was military interventions. Before military interventions regions were faring well. It takes time to undo the mistakes the military has done to this country. The democratic government has done well so far.

-Chief Emeka Anyaoku.

We are no longer ready to continue to tolerate poverty and broken promises from our government at the federal, state and local levels.

-Dr. Jibrin Ibrahim.

Tafawa Balewa was very young; Yakubu Gowon was very young: the late Zik was young and Awo too was young. They ruled this country at their primes; that was why they did so well in the first republic. That idea of recycling past leaders as if we the new generation have not come on board is not acceptable.

-Mr. Labaran Maku.

We had some people who were under 50years in leadership positions. The youngest was the Speaker..; you can still recall what happened to him…What .. did was not anything worse than what.. did.
We got them impeached. But in this part of the world some people covered up the other man. The man claimed he went to Government College, Ibadan but the governor.. went to Government College and packed all the documents so that they would not know that he did not   go   there.
I wanted someone who would succeed me so I took .. Within a year, I started seeing the type of man.. is. And you want me to get him there? I once went to Tanzania because Julius Nyerere recognised Biafra. He told me not to mind his aides and others in government. They would say they have one house in town but their five year old sons and daughters would have houses all over. Some of you who are condemning the leadership would get there tomorrow and it will be a different story. Only very few are actually good..Abacha, my predecessor got $750m. Through our lawyer in Switzerland we recovered $1.25bn and the lawyer still said there is probably still another $1bn to be recovered. In 1979 we had 20 new ships specially built for Nigeria. When I came back 20 years after, the national shipping line had liquidated. The whole thing is not just about leadership. If we talk about good leadership you should also talk about good followers. If you talk about human right you should also talk   about   human   duties   and   obligations.
It is sad that after ..years of independence we have no leader that we can commend. The problem in Africa is that when one person takes

over he would not see any good thing that his predecessor did. Let us condemn but with caution.

-Olusegun Obasanjo.

One of the greatest problems we have in our nation is that those who are supposed to be solutions to the problem of the nation are themselves part of the problem...If we are talking of changing Nigeria, we have to begin with ourselves.

-Rev. William Okoye.

By virtue of our size, our population, the ingenuity of our citizens their ability to endure, and the natural resources with which God in his mercy has endowed us, it is our fate to be great.

-- **Rev. William Okoye.**

We don't move at all, even after spending stupendous amount of money or recommendations of expert panels are treated with levity by the leaders and left to rot in archives...
Prosecution of high elite are never conclusive and if concluded the guilty ones are never punished, so as to achieve reformation or disincentive to corruption. The trustees of our common estate and wealth are given immunity by the inconclusive proceedings of the ICPC, EFCC, and the Public Service Tribunal. Why is it so? Justice delayed is justice denied. Maybe for fear or insecurity of their tenure, life or property. The processes are skewed to fail or are they hoping for "failings prescription," a Kangaroo Court for selective killing of leaders out of frustration and inability to crush corruption.

—**Maj-Gen I.B.M. Haruna (rtd), OFR.**

PART 3

INSPIRING THE NEW GENERATION

OF OUR PEOPLE PATRIOTIC VOICES OF UNITY AND REMEDY:

Criticisms may embarrass the country's leaders in the short-run, but strengthen their hands in the long-run; it may destroy a consensus of policy while expressing consensus of values.

-William Fulbright (Former American Senator).

Institutions develop and change not through fortuitous events or through some ..historical process, but through design and criticism and specifically criticism which proceeds from a skeptical outlook.

- Prof. B. Dudley.

First fool no be fool, second fool na him be proper foolish.

- Michael Okpara (foremost Nationalist).

Our enemies are the political profiteers, the swindlers, the men in high and low places that seek bribes and demand 10 percent; those that seek to keep the country divided permanently so that they can remain in office as ministers or VIPs at least, the tribalists, the nepotists, those that make the country look big for nothing before international circles, those that have corrupted our society and put the Nigerian political calendar back by their words and deeds.

-Maj. Nzeogwu.

We guarantee the security of life and property of all citizens in every part of Nigeria and equality in political rights. We also guarantee the right of every Nigerian to reside and work wherever he chooses in the Federation, as equal citizens of one united country. It is only right that we should all henceforth respect each other. We should all exercise civic restraint and use our freedom, taking into full account the legitimate right and needs of the other man. There is no question of second class citizenship in Nigeria…There is, therefore, no cause for humiliation on the part of any group of the people of this country…We.. should resolve our problems ourselves, free from foreign mentors and go-betweens however well intentioned. There is an urgent task to be done... We must restore at once to them hope and purpose in life.

-Yakubu Gowon, 15 Jan 1970.

My duty is to all citizens. I propose to treat all sections of the country with equality. The main obstacle to future stability in this country is the present structural imbalance in Nigeria.

-Gen. Yakubu Gowon (War-time Leader).

As you believe in your culture, village and your family, believe in the country. Let us from today make a way for the future generation to take over. We should ensure that the coming election is free, fair and credible by conducting ourselves in good manner. We should not engage ourselves on issues that could dilute the unity of the country.

—Gen. Yakubu Gowon, rtd.

Let us not make the mistake of thinking that this world is a prison. You are what you are for as long as it is comfortable for you. That is how I see it. I have continued to say that in Nigeria what we require is a nation that we can build together.

—Emeka Odumegwu Ojukwu.

It is only those who have not been involved in a war that will always push war as the first solution to any problem. War does not solve, it cowers but the problem remains.

—Emeka Odumegwu Ojukwu.

We are not so naive as to think that nationalism is a natural phenomenon, which comes about automatically, as we grow. It has not been so in any part of the world. National integration requires hard work. There is need for a dedicated leadership and citizenry imbued with faith to cultivate a wide-spread national feeling for "One Nigeria." I am convinced that these goals are attainable because we are at this time operating in more auspicious circumstances. Surely, we have learnt great lessons from the past and we have no need to permit divisive factors to continue to undermine our national well-being. I urge all Nigerians to join me in working with resolution for the attainment of these goals... There is need to transform our under-developed country into a modern industrialized society. To achieve this objective requires the energy of all of us. Our government is determined to release the creative energies of enterprising Nigerians and encourage them to help develop the economy for the good of all. I particularly call on the Labour Movement to rise up to the challenges of our time. ..the task ahead is enormous and it is a task for all of us. Our government is committed to building a united, stable and prosperous nation, I need your contribution, co-operation and support. Nigeria can and must become a great and modern nation. Let us with true conscience and determination join hands and re-dedicate ourselves to the service of this great country so that it will be a place we can and shall all be proud of. We cannot afford to fail in this task and by the grace of God, we shall succeed.

-Shehu Shagari, Oct 1, 1979.

The destiny of Nigeria is the destiny of 170 million of us. No single individual, no single tribe, religion, political party or region can usurp this destiny for its selfish whim. Our strength and unity is national, not regional.

—Mohammadu Buhari.

This country has had since independence a history mixed with turbulence and fortune. We have witnessed our rise to greatness, followed with a decline to the state of a bewildered nation. Our human potentials have been neglected, our natural resources put to waste. A phenomenon of constant insecurity and overbearing uncertainty has become characteristic of our national existence...This generation of Nigerians and indeed future generations have no other country but Nigeria. We must all stay and salvage it together. ..There is a lot of work to be done by every single Nigerian. Let us all dedicate ourselves to the cause of building a strong, united and viable nation for the sake of our own lives and the benefits of posterity.

-Maj-Gen Ibrahim Babangida, August 27, 1985.

I think we should forget about disintegration .., that can't happen in this country. It is not something that happens in one or two months. People say things to instill fear. If the majority of Nigerians believe in the unity of the country, then, why do they worry about someone saying it will disintegrate? I know it wouldn't. People are just crying wolf. Nigeria is one of the amazing countries we have in the world. If you live outside Nigeria and you hear and listen to all that, you will think the world is coming to an end. But, you need to come and see how Nigerian people are happy, laughing, attending matches and doing other things; that is Nigeria for you. When people say the nation would disintegrate, say "that will never happen."..there are still some leaders who believe in the unity of the country. You can't take it away and this is what we all believe in. So, anyone who believes in the unity of this country at any level is a leader. What we need is to follow leaders who have good intentions and understanding of what we want to achieve. We should also look for people who share the same view and work with them. That is how we will bring a strong leadership.

—Gen. Ibrahim Babangida.

New foundation must be laid..people are asking questions; people are confronting their leaders; people are asking for change and leadership that can turn around the fortune of this country.

—Gen . Ibrahim Babangida, rtd.

I believe Nigeria will survive and will be regarded as one of the great nations of the world. I believe that those who will be alive to witness the 100 years anniversary will appreciate what we are doing today.

—Gen. Abdusalami Abubakar, rtd.

As we are approaching the..general elections, there shouldn't be politics of bitterness regardless of tribal, partisan or religious differences. Nigerians should believe in the country, and politicians most play the game by the rules to make sure that the country progresses. You can't win all the time. Nigeria went through its own share of ups and downs; but we must realize that it's our collective responsibility to correct our mistakes and move the nation forward. Do not be led by the nose. Make sure that your votes count.

—Gen. Abdusalami Abubakar, rtd.

As we go for the next 50 years, we must take education as main priority. We must make sure that the younger generation got a very good blue print for the next 50 years.

—Gen. Abdusalami Abubakar, rtd.

Nigeria is wonderfully endowed by the Almighty with human and other resources.It does no credit either to us or the entire black race if we fail in managing our resources for quick improvement in the quality of life of our people. ..Fellow Nigerians, let us rise as one to face the task ahead and turn this daunting scene into opportunities in a new dawn. Let us make this the beginning of a genuine renaissance... It will be foolish to underrate the task ahead alone... With God as our guide and with 120 million Nigerians working with me with commitment, sustained effort and determination we shall not fail... Nobody, no matter who and where will be allowed to get away with the breach of the law or the perpetration of corruption and evil.

-Olusegun Obasanjo, May 29, 1999.

Nigerians have very little chance to make progress until there are enough citizens who are determined to put service to the society above their selfish interest.

- Olusegun Obasanjo.

Let's think well, let's say well, let's act well and Nigeria will move well.

-Olusegun Obasanjo.

My mission in government is largely to change the orientation of Nigerians from greed and corruption to serving the interest of the nation.

-Olusegun Obasanjo.

If Obasanjo could get there, Yar'Adua could get there and Jonathan can get there, any Nigerian can. It is now not a matter of the turn of any section or geographical area but the best interest of Nigeria and all Nigerians. It has been proved that no group – ethnic, linguistic, religious or geographical location – has monopoly of materials for leadership of our country. And no group solely by itself can crown any of it members the Nigerian CEO

—Olusegun Obasanjo.

With common identity as Nigerians, there is more that binds us than separates us. I am a Nigerian, born a Yoruba man, and I am proud of both identities, as they are for me complementary. Our duties, responsibilities and obligations to our country as citizens and, indeed, as leaders must go side by side with our rights and demands. There must be certain values and virtues that must go concomitantly with our dream… for me, my country I hold dear. .

—Olusegun Obasanjo.

On two occasions, I have had opportunity to work for my successors to the government of Nigeria. On both occasions, I never took the easy and destabilising route of ethnic, regional or religious consideration rather I took the enduring route of national, uniting and stabilising route. I worked for ..to succeed me not just because they are Moslems, Northerners or Hausa-Fulani, but also because they could strengthen the unity, stability and democracy in Nigeria. We incurred the displeasure of ethnic chauvinists for doing what was right for the country. That is in the nature of burden of leadership. A leader must lead no matter whose ox is gored… let national interest supersede personal or political feud and the machinations of satanic officials.

—Olusegun Obasanjo.

Don't always consider critics on national issues as enemies. Some of them may be as patriotic and nationalistic as you and I who had been in government. Some of them have as much passion for Nigeria as we have.. You must also differentiate between malevolent, mischievous and objective criticism. Analyses, criticisms and commentaries on government actions and policies are sinew of democracy.. May God save leaders from sycophants. They know what you want to hear and they feed you with it essentially for their own selfish interest. As far as.. and Nigeria are concerned, they are wreckers.. No interest should be higher or more important than Nigerian interest to… For me, there is neither North-South divide nor Christian-Moslem divide but one Nigeria.

—Olusegun Obasanjo.

I believe that with what Nigeria has gone through in the past, the worst should have already happened.. As I go around Nigeria and the world, I always come across Nigerians who are first-class citizens of the world and who are doing well where they are and who are passionate to do well for Nigeria. My hope for our country lies in these people. They abound and I hope that all of us will realize that they are the jewels of Nigeria wherever they may be and not those who arrogate to themselves eternal for ephemeral.

—Olusegun Obasanjo.

I will not support what I believe is not in the best interest of Nigeria, no matter who is putting it forward or who is behind it... In a democracy, leaders are elected to lighten the burden of the people, give them freedom, choice and equity and ensure good governance and not to deceive them, burden them, oppress them, render them hopeless and helpless. Nothing should be done to undermine the tenets, and values of democratic principles and practice. Tyranny in all its manifestation may be appealing to leader in trying times of political feud or disagreement. Democracy must, however, prevail and be held as sacrosanct.. Nigerians are no fools, they can see, they can hear, the can talk among themselves, they can think, they can compare and they can act in the interest of their country and in their own self-interest. They keenly watch all actions...

—Olusegun Obasanjo.

Fellow citizens, I ask you all to march with me into the age of restoration. Let us work together to restore our time-honoured value of honesty, decency, generosity, modesty, selflessness, transparency, and accountability. These fundamental values determine societies that succeed or fail. We must choose to succeed. I will set a worthy personal example as your President. No matter what obstacles confront us, I will set a worthy personal example as your President. I have confidence and faith in our ability to overcome them. After all, we are Nigerians! We are a resourceful and enterprising people, and we have it within us to make our country a better place. To that end I offer myself as a servant-leader. I will be a listener and doer, and serve with humility. To fulfil our ambitions, all our leaders at all levels whether a local government councillor or state governor, senator or cabinet minister must change our style and our attitude. We must act at all times with humility, courage, and forthrightness. I ask you, fellow citizens, to join me in rebuilding our Nigerian family, one that defines the success of one by the happiness of many. I ask you to set aside negative attitudes, and concentrate all our energies on getting to our common destination. All hands must be on deck. Let us join together to ease the pains of today while working for the gains of tomorrow. Let us set aside cynicism, and strive for the good society that we know is within our reach. Let us discard the habit of low expectations of ourselves as well as of our leaders. Let us stop justifying every shortcoming with that unacceptable phrase, "the Nigerian factor," as if to be a Nigerian is to settle for less. Let us recapture the mood of optimism that defined us at the dawn of independence, that legendary can-do spirit that marked our Nigerianness. Let us join together, now, to build a society worthy of our children. We have the talent. We have the intelligence. We have the ability. The challenge is great. The goal is clear. The time is now. I thank you, and God bless you.

-Umaru Musa Yar'adua, May 29, 2007.

We remember with pride, the nationalism and patriotism that inspired our founding fathers and the Nigerian people. They set aside their differences, to secure the unity and independence of our great country. That is the Nigerian spirit! For the Nigerian spirit cannot be broken. We are a resilient nation, determined to chart a course, through the turbulent waters of nation building. The Nigerian spirit is vibrant today in the world. Our citizens at home and abroad, are making their mark in all fields of human endeavour. These hard-working and committed Nigerians, remain a source of pride to us and a beacon of what is achievable, if we remain focused and determined.

--GEJ, October 1, 2011.

It is not about WHO will change Nigeria. It is how WE can change her instead. Nigeria is the sum of our thoughts and actions. I've trained myself not to think anything but positive thoughts about this great country of ours since God and the people of Nigeria gave me the opportunity to serve.

- GEJ, June 29, 2010.

Only team work can make the dream work. You and I are a team which is why I need to know what you think about the decisions of this administration. Communication rather than information is power. And I will listen to your voice. My vision is for Nigerians to be stake holders rather than onlookers in this administration.

-GEJ, June 30, 2010.

Athough government has made efforts to re-brand Nigeria's image, we all have to note that effective re branding must be a projection of things that are already happening. What does this mean? It means that the best way to tell the World that we are a 'good people' and a 'great nation' is to act it out in our daily lives. As I am never tired of saying, Nigeria is a sum of all of our thoughts and actions. And since our thoughts influence our actions, I would urge you to believe that we are indeed a good people and a great nation, think about it and it will influence how you act toward your country and country men and women. Please be under no illusion that outsiders will come in to do the work that has to be done to make Nigeria great. No. Take a look at the mirror and the image you will see is that of the person whose responsibility it is to make Nigeria great. So as we all wake up each day, let us each ask ourselves this question-how can I make Nigeria great today? The answer should be acted out in our locality. The effect of this local action would be felt nationally, and eventually noticed globally. It is at that point that others will believe it when we say 'Nigeria: Good people, great nation'.

-GEJ, July 27, 2010.

I know you are tired of empty promises, so I will make only one promise to you today... I call on you to join me to work together in harmony and synergy to forge a nation where we understand our differences instead of pretending they do not exist and work towards a perfect union founded on transparency, equity and justice. A nation that is on her way to repairing her International reputation and project to the world that things have changed and the people of

Nigeria have now taken Nigeria back from a few into the hands of her people who are eager, very eager to pull her weight in the forward movement of the African continent and the world in the pursuit of peace, prosperity and happiness...Please let us all unite across tongue and creed to move our long suffering nation forward together.

--GEJ, September 15, 2010

With patriotism and pragmatism, our founding fathers charted a course for the greatness of this country. While there were differences and disagreements, they did not waver in their desire to build a country that future generations would be proud of. They made compromises and sacrifices. They toiled night and day to build a viable country where progress and peace would reign supreme. Our independence was gained by men and women who envisioned a land of freedom and one of opportunity. Our founding fathers sought a government of character that seeks justice to her citizens, as our national anthem so eloquently describes: One Nation Bound in Freedom, Peace and Unity...Dear compatriots, despite the serious challenges that we have been living with; we cannot ignore the fact that we have cause to celebrate our nationhood and even a greater cause to look forward to a brighter future. This is a historic occasion when we need to pause and appreciate, who we are, what we have, and to reflect on the encouraging possibilities ahead. There is certainly much to celebrate: our freedom, our strength, our unity and our resilience. This is also a time for stock-taking, to consider our past so that it will inform our future. This is a time to look forward to the great opportunities and challenges that lie ahead for Nigeria... This should tell us something: that daunting as our circumstances have been, we are still full of ability and capability. We are blessed with talented and patriotic Nigerians at home and in the Diaspora... in our differences, tough circumstance and diversity, what binds us together is far stronger more than what divides us. We have a glorious future awaiting us. I am convinced that North or south, East or west, muslim, Christian or other faiths, majority or minority, we are all bound by our common humanity and mutual aspirations.

We are not sworn enemies. We are not irreconcilable foes. We are neighbours who sometimes offend each other but can always sit down to talk over differences. We are one people and one family...

Our faith maybe different. We may not speak the same language. We may not eat the same kind of food. But we are in a plural society where we have continued to accommodate one another and integrate without reservations. This we must build on! This we must strengthen! We have the opportunity of imitating our forefathers by envisioning a new society, where our children and children's children will live in peace and harmony and enjoy good quality of life comparable to the best the world can offer... We must reawaken in ourselves the hunger and aspirations of our founding fathers for a strong, united and prosperous nation that shall be the pride of future generations. To do this, we must change the old ways of doing things. The core values of patriotism, hard work, integrity and commitment to good governance must henceforth take precedence...It seems to me that the consensus of most Nigerians is that the time has come for us to break from the past and progress into a better future. We should not allow Nigeria to be pulled back again by those who believe it is either they have their way or the country should fall to pieces. The new Nigeria ahead of us, the new Nigeria we have to build together, is a society where everybody must feel at home. It must be a place we can all be happy, comfortable and confident to call our country. It is not just enough for us to talk about how Nigeria can be great; it is our duty to make Nigeria great. We can change Nigeria from our communities, cubicles and desks. The task to make Nigeria great is a task for every one…

The future of Nigeria and generations yet unborn is at stake... We must show the whole world that we can do things the right and the equitable way... We must have a new sense of purpose and a determination to make things work. We must collectively transform Nigeria...a new Nigeria is in the making. ..The great people of Nigeria, I implore all to join in the renewed efforts to remake Nigeria. It is a task for everyone. Pray for our country; wish our country well; do things that will make our country great; see and tap into opportunities for greatness that are everywhere around you and take pride in Nigeria. These are the ideals that I embrace. These are the issues that I am committed to. In conclusion, I will like to speak to Nigeria's greatest resource: our young men and women. I say you have the greatest stake in transforming our nation. It is time for this generation of Nigerians to answer the call and contribute to Nigeria's foundation of freedom. That is how this generation will make its mark. This is how we will make the most of these opportunities. That is how we will ensure that five decades from now, as our children and grand children celebrate our nation's independence centenary, we will be remembered as having contributed to the great history of Nigeria. On my part, I commit myself to doing my very best and to call on your intellect, wisdom and commitment to bring this dream to fruition.

--GEJ, October 1, 2010.

Nigeria is bigger than any individual or any collection of individuals. Nobody can hold a country of 150 million people to ransom any more. The interest of a few conceited, ill-motivated individuals cannot be bigger than our national aspirations... I believe that Nigerians have grown beyond this parochial mentality... On this mission, we cannot afford to fail. We will give our utmost, indeed our very best for the peace, unity and progress of Nigeria. May God Almighty bless Nigeria and stand with us

--GEJ, October 6, 2010.

There has grown over the years a tendency to think and believe that only things from foreign lands are good, modern or hip. Far from it. God has made all men and women good and with abilities to rise, stand or fall. The choice to rise, stand or fall resides in us. I have chosen to stand and rise with Nigerians for the good of our present and our future. Let me begin by saluting the creativity and excellence of our people all over the world who are setting the pace in education, culture and industry. For instance Nigerians are the most educated of any immigrant community in the U.S! This is a fact. Name any worthy honour such as the Nobel Prize, Booker Prize, Pulitzer Prize, Grammy Award, Olympic medal and what have you and a Nigerian has won it. What should that tell me and you? It tells us that we are among the very best of the very best on this planet. One of our most distinguished writers Chinualogu Achebe in his book the "Trouble with Nigeria" put the blame of our temporary situation on the door step of "leadership". I believe our revered Chinua Achebe is right. We must evolve a leadership that is avowedly committed to abolishing any form of human suffering in our society whether at the Community, local, State or Federal level of government. The era where leaders think only of their family, friends and associates alone must be a thing of the past. It is in this wise that I insisted that in our march towards consolidating our democracy leaders must emerge through a credible process of free and fair elections. Leaders must never be imposed...Nigeria can not have value beyond the value that Nigerians place on Nigeria and themselves. We need to soberly assess the value we place on ourselves because corporately we are what Nigeria is all about. Now if we place a low premium on ourselves as a people and on our culture, that translates to us placing a low premium on Nigeria. And the truth is that if we have priced ourselves low, we can not expect others to price us high. Our value and our sense of self worth is in our own hands. It is in how we see ourselves and our fellow citizens.

--GEJ, October 11, 2010.

Nigerians have to be their brothers' keeper. This should be above board because your brother is every Nigerian, not just those of the same religion, region or tribe as yourself.

--GEJ, October 14, 2010.

For a while now I have been talking on the theme of changing our attitude to Nigeria. ..if we want a different and better result for the next fifty years we have to do some things differently. In my opinion, the most important is this-as we enter into the next fifty years of our national existence, all of us, both the leaders and the led have to move from being onlookers to being stake holders in the Nigerian project. I have thought hard and long about this and I believe that we can only make this paradigm shift if we all and especially the leaders at all levels begin to assess our social services in Nigeria...me and celebrate brand Nigeria as we make it a habit to believe in Nigeria now and tomorrow. God bless Nigeria.

--GEJ, October 15, 2010.

Our movement is a mass movement in which all Nigerians have a stake and an equal presence. In this movement I see the triumph of nationalism, patriotism and the will to transform our economy and strengthen our collective security and wellbeing. I see in this movement a clear sign that as a people, we have broken free from sectional and diversionary sentiments and set our sights firmly on a common future. We have a program of action for the Government that will work with Nigerians to transform our country. Our movement will deliver a government that will bring proactive *peace and security*, private sector led ..development and coordinated ..*Development*. We will transform this country by improving the quality of *Education* to meet the requirements of the 21st century as shall be anchored on science, technology, innovation and a revitalization of our culture and values. The anti-corruption campaign will continue with additional emphasis on enhancing transparency and accountability in private and public sectors; complete ongoing investments in transport infrastructure and plan additional major investments. We will increase quality and number of housing by addressing housing financing and implement major reform in agriculture financing and land ownership. We will increase percentage of GDP from Solid Minerals Development ..within a reasonable time frame, and reform health care financing to improve infrastructure and services. Our vision is rooted in the realization that ..years after independence, our will as a people to share a common destiny is stronger than ever and our heart burns with yearning for a nation that will mobilize its human capital and resources to build a life of comfort for all her citizens. Our vision to build a nation that will be the pride of its people is the corner stone that drives our present mission... We are seeking a mandate to consolidate on our achievements and expand on additional commitments based on our vision for a greater Nigeria...I believe that we all have more to give to this movement. We welcome your ideas and your work in the field to strengthen and spread our message of transformation.

--GEJ, October 29, 2010.

The leadership of any nation is a highly coveted position and more so when that nation is Nigeria, the largest black nation on earth and so richly endowed with human and natural resources... For me, I care not about my personal safety, it is the safety and security of our citizens with regards to our age long aspirations to development and advancement that must be of concern. This election, I have said again and again is not about me, it is about Nigeria and the future of her great citizens... Since.. declaration millions of Nigerians around the world have formed citizens movements to canvass support for me. I want to say thank you to all Nigerians cutting across corporate, community, governmental, traditional, civic, youth and labour levels and various peoples movement, for your show of love and support. Expectedly the large following has also made me the target of lies, smear campaigns and innuendos. It is true that I do not own or have an interest in a newspaper, radio or television station and therefore my capacity to respond may not be as robust and swift as those who control these mass media however, I thank God that we have men and women of conscience who also work in these media institutions who love Nigeria and can do what is right. I thank them for towing a different path away from the hurricane of negativism in the polity…because they want to stop a change whose time has come.

--GEJ, November 1, 2010.

By my nature and upbringing, desperation is not one of my credentials. The Presidency of Nigeria is a national and treasured asset and only God and the people must decide who leads the project of protecting and advancing her interest. So when you hear or read falsehoods .. and such other stories that enter the fertile minds of the mischievous you must know that their desperation is getting to fever pitch levels and their project of self-agenda is ready to anchor on the harbour of the-more- of- the same. We must not allow them to confuse the issues that are of concern to Nigerians: Proactive peace and security; Major reform in Agriculture that will empower farmers and make food available so that no child of Nigeria can go to bed hungry; Available, accessible, affordable electric power to power our idle industries and create jobs; Niger Delta Development so that the many decades of strife in the region can be brought to a peaceful and happy end; Improved quality education that will be anchored on science, technology, innovation and a revitalisation of our cultural and literary resources.

--GEJ, November 1, 2010.

We must be concerned about fighting corruption with additional emphasis on enhancing transparency and accountability and focusing attention on addressing the housing needs of our people and growing the solid mineral sector and investment in road and transport infrastructure to wean us of our over dependence on oil and gas. I am not and will not be interested in the gutter fight of blackmail, sectionalism and promoting regional interest over national interest.

--GEJ, November 1, 2010.

I want to appeal to you ..that when you hear or read of attacks on me or any other candidate, please be patriotic enough to resist the temptation of joining them to trivialise the presidential race. I urge you to very gently ask the purveyors of such fanciful tales of degradation to rather tell you about their plans for Nigeria as I have done. If they have plans then they ought to run on them. If they do not it means that they have none and it is trite knowledge that those who have no plan, plan only to fail and Nigeria and Nigerians in whatever conditions are no failures!

--GEJ, November 1, 2010.

So ..fellow Nigerians, as the race heats up I promise you I will remain steadfast and continue to work for our country and fulfil my promise of "promising less and delivering more". All uncompleted projects in the power sector will be completed and commissioned; all projects that have a direct bearing on your lives and those that of fundamental importance to steering the ship of state aright towards the destination of unity and greatness will be sustained. I want to earn your vote not through mudslinging or blackmail. I want to earn your vote through performance and the realisation of a promise that through me every Nigeria regardless of circumstances of birth, state of origin, parental background, access to power and money can contribute his or her little quota to the unity and progress of our beloved Nation

--GEJ, November 1, 2010.

I want to assure the people of..and the rest of Nigeria that this is what I meant when I made a commitment to promise Less and deliver More. I would rather demonstrate what we are doing by working quietly and let you see the results than talk about it... I have committed myself to be a father that does not show favouritism and I am very committed to make sure that there is development of every part of Nigeria. There is development coming and I am committed to making it happen.

--GEJ, November 3, 2010.

I had earlier in a note entitled 'Farewell to Do or Die Elections' ..to the larger Nigerian society pledged my willingness to play politics without pain...we believe in persuasion over coercion... Contrary to what those with ulterior motives will want us to believe..our beloved country Nigeria will remain. ..I.. do not subscribe to the politics of rancour and recriminations or do or die and coercion. And as long as God keeps me, I will never permit any agency of the Federal Government to be used for the purpose of circumventing the will of the Nigerian people.

--GEJ, November 11, 2010.

I want to assure you .. that the only consensus that will matter ..is the consensus of the Nigerian people as displayed in a free and fair election. I believe this and this is why our campaign team and I will campaign to you on ideas, issues, plans and things already delivered. We will never campaign on the basis of tribe, region, religion and personal attacks. I am reminded at this stage of a lesson taught to me by a learned professor of mine while I was at the university. He said "great minds talk about ideas, minds on the way to greatness talk about things, but small minds talk about people and where they are from rather than where they are going".

--GEJ, November 11, 2010.

You, me and everybody else has no control over where we come from, only God does. Rather we have control over where we are going? Today, I ask Nigerians to make a choice. Would you rather talk about where an aspirant is from or where he/she is going?

--GEJ, November 11, 2010.

Our administration intends to tackle the issue of insecurity holistically rather than reacting in a knee jerk manner. I had said we will pay special attention on preventive strategies even as we focus on equipping and training our personnel to secure our nation. You may recall that I had traced the root of insecurity to poverty and that poverty has a very stubborn relationship to illiteracy. Now I am not unmindful of the fact that even where some of our youths would want to be educated, we simply do not have enough facilities to educate all our people up to university level at present...I am one of those who believe that a nation will not get rich by merely exploiting its natural resources rather wealth will come from exposing it's human resources to knowledge and values of community spirit.

--GEJ, November 15, 2010.

Many youths may not recall the labours of our heroes past and this is one reason why I want our educational system to revive and promote the study of Civics and Ethics as a part of Social Studies in our Primary schools curriculum...We must celebrate our own heroes and by so doing encourage the youth to aspire to be like them knowing that their efforts will not be in vain. It is elementary knowledge that whatever you appreciate increases in value. And I..choose to appreciate our heroes irrespective of region and religion. I also recommend this attitude to all and sundry so that when our youth sing our National Anthem and say "to serve with heart and might one nation bound in freedom, peace and unity" they can see that being lived out in the lives of those of us who are priviledged to serve our nation.

--GEJ, November 17, 2010.

Nigerians should know that I and the administration I lead feel their pains...and that we must work together to build real consensus that takes the whole nation into consideration not just a section...able to build a consensus that aims to move the nation forward. I as President am a bridge builder and I will always strive to include not exclude.

--GEJ, November 27, 2010.

I have congratulated.. not because I am glad my party lost, but because I believe firmly and fundamentally in the rule of law. As President, I have a covenant with my Creator and Nigerians to uphold the rule of law and insist that the right thing be done at all times. Having said that, I find it sad that any member of our party will express happiness over our party's loss.. This thing called loyalty cannot be bought in the market. As I said before, in our service in life whether to our family, to Nigeria, to our political party and to our friends, Loyalty is that essential ingredient that sweetens the soup of relationships and togetherness. It must be one for all and all for one... while I do not want to drag you into partisan politics, the challenge before us all is to help grow our democracy by working to perfect and strenthen the vehicles and institutions of our democractic enterprise.

--GEJ, November 28, 2010.

We cannot surender our economy to smugglers. Our goal is to empower our people as we embark on this journey of self-suficiency and economic ascendancy. Pending when our initiatives come on stream we have decided to adopt a multi-pronged approach to stemming the billions we lose to unpatriotic persons and also support the rise of local industry by providing the needed incentives for local production and discourging smuggling.

--GEJ, December 3, 2010.

My Brothers and Sisters, it is no more news that our country was viciously attacked on both Christmas and New Years eves by terrorists who want to manipulate the fate of Nigeria as we approach an epochal year of positive change. They spoke to all Nigerians through bombs, deaths, violence and destruction. There was no national interest reason for them to speak that way. I want to assure whoever they are that Nigeria and Nigerians will speak to them firmly, effectively and in a manner our present laws allows. We will take justice to them wherever they are hiding for our nation's peace and security cannot be sacrificed on the altar of narrow interest... I repeat: they have spoken through deaths and messages of sorrow, now Nigerians will speak through love, unity and justice. It is the intention of those behind the blast to get government and Nigerians to enter into panic mode and begin to react instead of proact. If we do this they have won. So we have to take all necessary steps to bring them to book after swift but thorough investigations while we also allow for no disruption in our plans for a prosperous new year...I know that we have been through trying times... I know that there have been people who have lost loved ones, people who have gone to bed hungry, people who have had to drop out of school and people who have lost jobs... To these people, I say be hopeful and believe that Nigeria will be better off ..because this administration has put a lot of thought into making plans that it intends to bring to fruition God helping us and with the cooperation of the National Assembly and the Nigerian people.

--GEJ, January 2, 2011.

I asked for your trust so that we can continue to expand the political space, promote greater democratic culture and unite our nation for rapid progress and speedy transformation... we have witnessed a campaign of unusual intensity within an unconstrained political space... our people have chosen the unity of our country above all other considerations. It is a quantum leap into the great ideals to hold our great nation together. I promise all Nigerians that I will within my powers not disappoint this umbrella of unity you have entrusted on me today. I will carry this banner to all the corners of our great country to make sure that the essence of this unity is not lost on our people...This victory is not for me alone... It is a victory for ..indeed all Nigerians because it takes us one step closer to the Nigerian dream of national transformation. ..I want to welcome ..on board so that together we can build a Nigeria of our collective interest. A Nigeria where ideas guide our dreams for a greater nation...This country has many challenges and our polity certainly needs reform. Our economy needs to be strengthened, opportunities need to be spread and security needs to be improved.

--GEJ, January 13, 2011.

Only a national..can lead us through the national transformation Nigeria needs. ..These are uncommon times in the history of this country. The challenges that confront this country are enormous but the opportunities available to us are even more. It is our responsibility..to listen to Nigerians and move in the direction that the people expect us to go...Nigerians want peace and security and we are determine to provide it...We are shedding the politics and corruption of the past that has held us down for too long and have formulated the strategy and team to transform Nigeria. It won't always be easy, but our momentum is strong and our vision for Nigeria is clear: through an improved power sector, stronger educational system, better security, and policies that promote Nigerian business development and jobs. Nigeria will play big globally as we approach the year...Nigeria has the talent, skill, determination and passion to reach this ambitious - but achievable - goal. And our administration..has the right priorities and strategy to make it happen.

--GEJ, January 13, 2011.

In a time of active politicking, when scoring political points have taken precedence over our overarching goal of nation building, we must not allow those strong bonds which tie us together as a nation, and which brought our people to the streets, for the common cause of seeing that the right thing is done by all and for all the people of our country..to be dispensed with by the mere nuance which we attach to words.. .as .. I move around the country seeking the mandate of our dear countrymen and women, we shall continue to respect and pay tribute to the hard work and patience of all our people. Our promise of a significant turnaround in the way our country operates and is governed is an article of faith. I made a commitment to Nigerians that our campaign will be about issues and livelihood advancement. I am determined to remain true to this commitment.

--GEJ, February 14, 2011.

We made the promise and will zealously deliver on, amongst other things, a stable, constant supply of electricity which will revolutionise the way business is done in our country.We will pay special attention to the security of lives and property; we will focus on access to good quality health andeducation for all Nigerians and job creation for our youths, for this is the only way we can defeat poverty.

--GEJ, February 14, 2011.

We are focused on delivering on our commitment to agricultural and infrastructural development, the expansion of our economy and the complete transformation of our national security architecture in other to better secure lives and property in our Country. Let us all insist in building a united nation where justice, equity and the fundamental essence of freedom and democracy is sustained.

--GEJ, February 14, 2011.

I have been going round Nigeria, State to State and City to City. My God, Nigeria is beautiful! I have been talking about our plans to improve our ailing infrastructure, our education standards, Power, Agriculture and the health sector among others. I have been telling Nigerians who gather in their thousands in Bauchi, Jos, Ilorin, Minna, Port Harcourt, Owerri, Ibadan, Kaduna, Lafia and others that the most urgent thing we need to do is to create jobs for our youths and develop our country and this we have started to do with progress being made...I have been telling Nigerians that we will build a greater union that generations yet unborn will be proud of by focusing on social justice and levelling the playing field and empowering people to be all that God has put in them to be. Many may not appreciate that it is a privilege to be born a Nigerian. It is even a greater privilege that one is called to lead such a bold, brilliant and most enterprising people in one of the most blessed land on earth.

--GEJ, February 24, 2011.

Going through Nigeria and seeing the beautiful land and comely faces of Nigerians reminds me of this song that used to play on the NTA in the eighties. Join me and sing it if you remember the melody; *I love Nigeria, I no go lie, Na inside am I go live and die.*

--GEJ, February 24, 2011.

The promise I give to you..Nigerians is that my uncommon story made possible by God and the Nigerian people be the story that every child of Nigeria can become a part. It is my determination to ensure that no Nigerian child goes to bed hungry or goes to school without shoes or school bags to put his or her books in when he or she takes those promising steps to school. The time for transformation is now... I have no choice but to work hard to make the Nigeria of our dream come true. I have no where to go. Anything that I ever own in life is in Nigeria. Please join me in prayers as we continue the conversation for transformation across our great country.

--GEJ, February 24, 2011.

Public office to me is not a means to adding value to the holder of the office. Public office is the vehicle through which social harmony, happiness and inspirational communal existence is promoted and enhanced. I personally do not believe that you become a 'big man' by simply holding a public office. No! People with that type of mentality are only borrowing moral authority from the office they occupy and as soon as they leave that office that authority leaves them...I believe that public office is a pedestal for you to use your strength of character to add value to the office by serving the people you are meant to serve and giving glory to our Creator.

--GEJ, February 28, 2011.

Some people accuse me of being humble to the point of servility. They do not understand that the whole purpose of public office is to serve. This is why our late great leader, Umaru Musa Yar'adua said that we were servant leaders. We have not come to demand service from Nigeria but to give service... I am acutely aware that I do not hold this position of President of the Federal Republic of Nigeria by the wishes of any power other than the freely given mandate of the Nigerian people and the grace of God. And that is why I communicate with you because next to the Almighty God, the Nigerian people are my power source and just as an electrical appliance will not work when not connected to its power source so also can I not work effectively if I am not connected with you the good people of Nigeria.

--GEJ, February 28, 2011.

And while there are politicians who have substantial commitment to Nigeria and others who may have partial commitment to Nigeria, my commitment to Nigeria is total and there is evidence to back it up. It is believed that a man's greatest treasures are his children and immediate family and the proverb goes that where a man's treasures are there his heart also will be. All my children, every last one of them school in Nigeria and of course my wife and I are fully on the ground. Some might describe other treasures a man has as his real estate property. And again every property I have in life is in Nigeria. Some might consider money as another treasure and again all my accounts every last one of them is domiciled in Nigeria. In everything I do I make a conscious decision to put Nigeria first whether it is in my dressing or the food I eat, or even the music I listen to. I am totally sold out on Nigeria. What does this tell you? My commitment to Nigeria is not partial, neither is it substantial, but it is total. You can trust me to take good decisions on behalf of Nigeria because I am a stakeholder whose progress is tied to the progress of Nigeria. This is the core of who Goodluck Ebele Jonathan is. I have made myself an open book, completely transparent to Nigerians because I want to earn your trust. I do not want to demand trust, but I want to inspire it by the way I live my life and with your help and God's favour I shall continue to do this.

--GEJ, February 28, 2011.

My dear brothers and sisters, today it is independence day for Nigeria yet again. Together we have said yes to one Nigeria. Together we have agreed to be our brother's keeper. Together we have spoken with one voice to say no to dichotomy. Together we have chosen a rebirth...Together we shall win forever!
"this generation of Nigerians and indeed future generations have no other country than Nigeria. We shall remain here and salvage it TOGETHER"...in a contest amongst brothers "there is no victor nor vanquished". We are all Nigerians and today all Nigerians are winners because we now know that North, South, East or West, Nigeria is best!

--GEJ, April 18, 2011.

This administration had taken practical steps to ensure the attainment of its goal of delivering free, fair and credible elections...Sadly, some misguided elements do not share in the spirit of our democratic achievements. They formed into groups of miscreants and struck with deadly and destructive force in some parts of the country...They killed and maimed innocent citizens. They set ablaze business premises, private homes and even places of worship. In some cases, they showed utter disrespect to all forms of authority, including our most revered traditional institutions. They systematically targeted population groups. They singled out and harassed nationalistic politicians. They intimidated travellers...They waylaid vulnerable Youth Corps members, even though we all know that these young and innocent Nigerians are guests within our communities and are agents of public good and national unity. We are shocked by these horrific acts which strike at the heart of our nation. These disturbances are more than mere political protests. Clearly, they aim to frustrate the remaining elections. This is not acceptable. If anything at all, these acts of mayhem are sad reminders of the events which plunged our country into 30 months of an unfortunate civil war. As a nation, we are yet to come to terms with the level of human suffering, destruction and displacement, including that of our children to far-away countries, occasioned by those dark days. In recent years, we have also witnessed other acts of intolerance, violence and destruction of human life perpetrated by unpatriotic elements for no justifiable reason. Indeed, the nation still bears some of the scars of other similar events like the aftermath of the June 12 1993 elections that brought our polity to the brink. It is inconceivable therefore, that there are some in our midst who seek to re-enact a stalemate in the political process.My fellow countrymen and women, ENOUGH IS ENOUGH.

--GEJ, February 21, 2011.

Democracy is about the rule of law. It is to its credit, that in recent years our judiciary has demonstrated great courage, fortitude and independence in the discharge of its duties. There are, therefore, no grievances that our laws and courts cannot address...As president, it is my solemn duty to defend the constitution of this country. That includes the obligation to protect the lives and properties of every Nigerian wherever they choose to live. I will defend the right of all citizens to freely express their democratic choice anywhere in this country; to enjoy every freedom and opportunity that this country can offer without let or hindrance.

--GEJ, February 21, 2011.

To those who persist in sowing the seeds of discord, I say, you may hurt and bring grief to some innocent families momentarily, but you will never succeed in stopping our transformational journey: a journey that will lead this country, by the grace of God, to emerge stronger, more prosperous and more united. Dear brothers and sisters, let us continue to build a nation in which we all live in peace. A nation where the bonds of our common aspirations and goals will spur and re-energise our resolve towards greatness. A nation where our children from North and South, East and West will grow with hope and live together as brothers, sisters and friends. Let us always remember that we are all part of a shared destiny.

--GEJ, February 21, 2011.

We have made an investment into our future by voting in leaders at all levels over the past month. Now let us make a further investment in belief... but for Nigeria to work at her optimal best there is need for everyone of us to believe in Nigeria and work as a team because irrespective of the outcome of..elections, my outlook has and shall continue to be that in a contest amongst brothers there will be no victor and no vanquished. We must all make a paradigm shift to a win/win mentality. When we do, we will of necessity change the conversation from-how will President .. change Nigeria-to-how will I the Nigerian worker .. change Nigeria? ... I ask that you and the government work as a team to achieve this.

--GEJ, May 2, 2011.

Let no one be in doubt, there is work ahead of us. It is not going to be a party, rather it will be a case of rolling up our sleeves and getting to work ...one of my desires for Nigeria is that the growth of our economy should be driven by the production of our people and this will only happen when we make a substantial investment in the Nigerian people by way of increasing access to and the quality of education, working with the Private Sector to improve on electricity generation and distribution and motivating our workers by ensuring that the New Minimum Wage as enshrined in the Minimum Wage Act is implemented throughout the length and breadth of Nigeria.

--GEJ, May 2, 2011.

While I am not perfect, I can state with a clear conscience that there has been progress...I have stated all these to give you a sense that commitments freely entered into by this administration which I lead will be kept as much as is humanly possible as I am keen to build trust between government and the governed. Thus, I assure you that I as President will channel all the resources available to the Federal Government to meeting every promise I made to Nigerians during the Presidential campaigns... I therefore thank you for giving me and my team the opportunity to preside over the affairs of Nigeria for the last year and rededicate myself to the service of Nigeria so help me God.

--GEJ, May 6, 2011.

During the campaigns, one of the things I noticed in my tours all over Nigeria is the income disparity amongst the geo-political zones. I am not comfortable with disparity and I am committed to use every means possible to change the situation. Now I requested for and studied data on the income disparity amongst our zones and was able to determine that the zones with the highest level of education have the highest GDP and Per Capita Income and it was therefore a no brainer that the key to upward mobility in income is education. This is the reason why I have focused on education almost to the point of obsession.

--GEJ, May 18, 2011.

As I have often said, my approach to solving issues has always been by beginning with the end in mind. Yes, it may be expected by some that we should throw money at the problem, but I am convinced that that is only giving fish to the hungry. To solve the income disparity issues in Nigeria, I am convinced that it is better to teach Nigerians to fish.

--GEJ, May 18, 2011.

I also wish to pay tribute our founding fathers, whose enduring sacrifices and abiding faith in the unity and greatness of our country, laid the foundation for the nation. We take enormous pride in their contributions. The pivotal task of this generation is to lift our fatherland to the summit of greatness..earlier this year, over seventy-three million eligible Nigerians endured all manner of inconvenience just to secure their voters cards, in order to exercise the right to choose those that will govern them... we saw the most dramatic expressions of the hunger for democracy. Stories of courage and patriotism were repeated in many ways.. The inspiring story . . across the country, who struggled against the physical limitations of age to cast their vote, is noteworthy. Such determination derives from the typical Nigerian spirit of resilience in the face of the greatest of odds. That spirit has, over the years, stirred our hopes, doused our fears, and encouraged us to gather ourselves to build a strong nation even when others doubted our capacity.

--GEJ, May 29, 2011.

Today, our unity is firm, and our purpose is strong. Our determination unshakable. Together, we will unite our nation and improve the living standards of all our peoples whether in the North or in the South; in the East or in the West. Our decade of development has begun. The march is on. The day of transformation begins today. We will not allow anyone exploit differences in creed or tongue, to set us one against another.

--GEJ, May 29, 2011.

I am mindful that I represent the shared aspiration of all our people to forge a united Nigeria: a land of justice, opportunity and plenty, Confident that a people that are truly committed to a noble ideal, cannot be denied the realization of their vision. I assure you that this dream of Nigeria that is so deeply felt by millions will indeed come to reality.

--GEJ, May 29, 2011.

A decade ago, it would have been a mere daydream to think that a citizen from a minority ethnic group could galvanize national support, on an unprecedented scale, to discard ancient prejudices, and win the people's mandate as President of our beloved country. That result emanated from the toil and sacrifice of innumerable individuals and institutions, many of whom may never get to receive public appreciation for their effort.

--GEJ, May 29, 2011.

In the days ahead, those of us that you have elected to serve must show that we are men and women with the patriotism and passion, to match the hopes and aspirations of you, the greater people of this country. We must demonstrate the leadership, statesmanship, vision, capacity, and sacrifice, to transform our nation. We must strengthen common grounds, develop new areas of understanding and collaboration, and seek fresh ideas that will enrich our national consensus. It is the supreme task of this generation to give hope to the hopeless, strength to the weak and protection to the defenceless.

--GEJ, May 29, 2011.

Fellow citizens, the leadership we have pledged is decidedly transformative. The transformation will be achieved in all the critical sectors, by harnessing the creative energies of our people. We must grow the economy, create jobs, and generate enduring happiness for our people. I have great confidence in the ability of Nigerians to transform this country. The urgent task of my administration is to provide a suitable environment, for productive activities to flourish. I therefore call on the good people of Nigeria, to enlist as agents of this great transformation.

--GEJ, May 29, 2011.

My dear countrymen and women, being a Nigerian is a blessing. It is also a great responsibility. We must make a vow that, together, we will make the Nigerian Enterprise thrive. The leadership and the followership must strive to convert our vast human and natural resources into the force that leads to a great Nigeria. The Nigeria of our dreams must be built on handwork and not on short cuts.

--GEJ, May 29, 2011.

Let me salute the Nigerian workers who build our communities, cities and country. They deserve fair rewards, and so do the women that raise our children, and the rural dwellers that grow our food. The moment is right. The signs are heart-warming. We are ready to take off on the path of sustained growth and economic development.

--GEJ, May 29, 2011.

We will push programs and policies that will benefit both local and foreign businesses, but we must emphasize mutual benefits and win-win relationships…Fellow citizens, in every decision, I shall always place the common good before all else. The bane of corruption shall be met by the overwhelming force of our collective determination, to rid our nation of this scourge. The fight against corruption is a war in which we must all enlist, so that the limited resources of this nation will be used for the growth of our common wealth.

--**GEJ, May 29, 2011.**

I am confident that we have every reason to look to the future with hope. We owe ourselves and posterity the duty of making this country respectable in the comity of nations. Nigeria, as a responsible member of the international community, will remain committed to the maintenance of global peace and security. We will continue to play an active role in the United Nations. Our role in the African Union, ECOWAS, and the Gulf of Guinea will be enhanced to ensure greater human and energy security.

--**GEJ, May 29, 2011.**

My fellow countrymen and women, Nigerian is not just a land of promise; it shall be a nation where positive change will continue to take place, for the good of our people. The time for lamentation is over. This is the era of transformation. This is the time for action. But Nigerian can only be transformed if we all play our parts with commitment and sincerity. Cynicism and skepticism will not help our journey to greatness. Let us all believe in a new Nigerian. Let us work together to build a great country that we will all be proud of. ..Fellow Compatriots, lift your gaze towards the horizon. Look ahead and you will see a great future that we can secure with unity, hard work and collective sacrifice.

--**GEJ, May 29, 2011.**

Join me now as we begin the journey of transforming Nigeria: I will continue to fight, for your future, because I am one of you. I will continue to fight, for improved medical care for all our citizens I will continue to fight for all citizens to have access to first class education. I will continue to fight, for electricity to be available to all our citizens. I will continue to fight, for an efficient and affordable public transport system for all our people. I will continue to fight for jobs to be created through productive partnerships.

--**GEJ, May 29, 2011.**

You have trusted me with your mandate, and I will never, never let you down. I know your pain, because I have been there. Look beyond the hardship you have endured. See a new beginning, a new direction; a new spirit. Nigerians, I want you to start to dream again. What you see in your dreams, we can achieve together. ..Let us work together, let us build together, let us bequeath a greater Nigeria to the generations   to   come.

--GEJ, May 29, 2011.

I value all Nigerians. I see our youth who are looking for jobs and yet remain hopeful. I see the farmer, and fisherman, toiling everyday to earn a living. I see the teacher, working hard, to train our future generations, with much sacrifice. I see the market women whose entrepreneurial spirit helps to generate income for their children and families. I see our sportsmen and women training hard to bring glory to our nation. I see our resilience and commitment, as a nation, to defend our democracy and secure our future. I see every single profession and vocation, making positive contributions to national progress. I value you all!

--GEJ, October 1, 2011.

Together, we shall work for a Nigeria in which democracy and the rule of law are sacrosanct. A country where corruption and its attendant vices are banished. A country where human life is sacred and respected, and where the rights of the individual are protected. Nigeria is a young entity in the comity of nations and yet in her .. years, she has made significant strides in making her presence felt all over the world. The journey to nationhood always has its own challenges. Nigeria has had her own share. Our growing pains as a nation have included the civil war, the June 12 election crisis and restlessness in the Niger Delta. But Nigeria has always overcome each of these challenges. We overcame before. We will overcome yet again.

--GEJ, October 1, 2011.

Today, as a nation, there is much for us to celebrate. We celebrate our diversity. We celebrate our entrepreneurial spirit. We celebrate our resilience and ability to turn adversity into hope. We celebrate our culture. For the labours of our heroes past, shall never be in vain... let me reassure all Nigerians that I remain resolutely committed to the ideals and dreams of our founding fathers. Let me also reassure Nigerians that I will strongly defend the peace and stability of our nation.

--GEJ, October 1, 2011.

We condemn all acts of violence and declare that such acts of mindless savagery shall not be allowed to define our country. We will not be deterred. Our resolve is strong. . . no matter what we do as your elected leaders, at all levels, the peace and security of our nation rest also on our collective efforts as citizens, in our various communities.

--GEJ, October 1, 2011.

We must manage our resources more prudently and efficiently... I call on our political leaders to put aside partisan politics, for united action towards the advancement of our nation. We must build together... Our potential is huge. ..Already, we are beginning to do things differently. I believe that integrity, honour, patriotism, selfless service and fear of God, must be the hallmarks of leadership at all levels.

--GEJ, October 1, 2011.

A nation is sustained by its institutions and systems. .. Let me assure all Nigerians of my resolve to lead our nation into a safer, more peaceful, and prosperous future for our children. .. For the time has come, to rise above ethnic and religious divisions; The time has come, to unite against violence, in all its ramifications; The time has come, to secure our peace, and unite against suffering, and deprivation; I see a new Nigeria rising. A Nigeria, that is economically strong. A Nigeria, that takes its rightful place of leadership in the world. A Nigeria, that uses its diversity to reinforce its strength. A Nigeria, we all can be proud of. .. This is the Nigeria we need and this is the Nigeria, we all must build... let us resolve to build the Nigeria of our future.

--GEJ, October 1, 2011.

This government will lead Nigeria and Nigerians to resist imposition. We must not allow the activities of violent individuals to define the year ... Many years from today the story of our democratic and survival enterprise will record the year . . as a turning point. . .This is what I promised Nigerians when I campaigned for their votes-Transformation. And I have not just concerned myself with growth indices such as these, but this administration has taken steps to make sure that these growth indices trickle down to the grass roots in the form of development indices...I look forward to a year where we would begin the consolidation of our economic and fiscal reforms and direct more resources to capital expenditure. I look forward to a year where our efforts at reforming the education sector would yield fruit in the form of an increased pass rate in our school leaving examinations. But most of all, I look forward to a year of all of us working together in peace and harmony to live up to the Nigerian Vision of our founding fathers of a nation which finds unity and strength in her diversity... May God bless you and the Federal Republic of Nigeria.

--GEJ, January 1, 2012.

I urge all Nigerians to eschew bitterness and acrimony and live together in harmony and peace. Wherever there is any threat to public peace, our security agencies will enforce the law, without fear or favour...Let me seize this opportunity to assure all Nigerians that I feel the pain that you all feel. I personally feel pained to see the sharp increase in transport fares and the prices of goods and services. I share the anguish of all persons who had travelled out of their stations, who had to pay more on the return leg of their journeys. If I were not here to lead the process of national renewal, if I were in your shoes at this moment, I probably would have reacted in the same manner as some of our compatriots, or hold the same critical views about government. But I need to use this opportunity as your President to address Nigerians on the realities on the ground, and why we chose to act as we did. I know that these are not easy times.

But tough choices have to be made to safeguard the economy and our collective survival as a nation.

--GEJ, January 7, 2012.

My fellow Nigerians, the truth is that we are all faced with two basic choices with regard to the management of the downstream petroleum sector: either we deregulate and survive economically, or we continue with a subsidy regime that will continue to undermine our economy and potential for growth, and face serious consequences. As you all know, the subject of deregulation is not new, we have been grappling with it for more than two decades. Previous administrations tinkered with the pump price of petroleum products, and were unable to effect complete deregulation of the downstream sector. This approach has not worked. If it did, we would not be here talking about deregulation today. I understand fully well that deregulation is not a magic formula that will address every economic challenge, but it provides a good entry point for transforming the economy, and for ensuring transparency and competitiveness in the oil industry, which is the mainstay of our economy. As a President, elected and supported by ordinary Nigerians, and the vast majority of our people, I have a duty to bring up policies and programmes that will grow the economy and bring about greater benefits for the people. Let me assure you that as your President, I have no intention to inflict pain on Nigerians. The deregulation of the petroleum sector is a necessary step that we had to take. Should we continue to do things the same way, and face more serious economic challenges? Or deregulate, endure the initial discomfort and reap better benefits later? I want to assure every Nigerian that whatever pain you may feel at the moment, will be temporary.

--GEJ, January 7, 2012.

The interest of the ordinary people of this country will always remain topmost in my priorities as a leader. I remain passionately committed to achieving significant and enduring improvements in our economy that will lead to sustained improvement in the lives of our people. I am determined to leave behind a better Nigeria, that we all can be proud of. To do so, I must make sure that we have the resources and the means to grow our economy to be resilient, and to sustain improved livelihood for our people. We must act in the public interest, no matter how tough, for the pains of today cannot be compared to the benefits of tomorrow. On assumption of office as President, I swore to an oath to always act in the best interest of the people. I remain faithful to that undertaking.

--GEJ, January 7, 2012.

To save Nigeria, we must all be prepared to make sacrifices. On the part of Government, we are taking several measures aimed at cutting the size and cost of governance, including on-going and continuous effort to reduce the size of our recurrent expenditure and increase capital spending. In this regard, I have directed that overseas travels by all political office holders, including the President, should be reduced to the barest minimum. The size of delegations on foreign trips will also be drastically reduced; only trips that are absolutely necessary will be approved.

--GEJ, January 7, 2012.

We are all greatly concerned about the issue of corruption. The deregulation policy is the strongest measure to tackle this challenge in the downstream sector.. .Government will be vigilant and act decisively to curb the excesses of those that want to exploit the current situation for selfish gains. I plead for the understanding of all Nigerians. I appeal to our youth not to allow mischief-makers to exploit present circumstances to mislead or incite them to disturb public peace.

--GEJ, January 7, 2012.

Government has taken . . decisions in the best interest of our economy, so that we not only have benefits today, but to ensure that we bequeath even greater benefits to our children and grandchildren. Let me assure Nigerians that every possible effort will be made to ensure that we march forward, with a collective resolve to build a Nigeria that can generate greater economic growth, create and sustain new jobs, and secure the future of our children.

--GEJ, January 7, 2012.

Let me assure you that government will continue to respect the people's right to express themselves within the confines of the law and in accordance with the dictates of our democratic space. ..Let me assure Nigerians that this administration is irrevocably committed to tackling corruption...I urge you to show understanding. . and give government your full support ... Government will not condone brazen acts of criminality and subversion. As President, I have sworn to uphold the unity, peace and order of the Nigerian State and by the grace of God, I intend to fully and effectively discharge that responsibility...Nigeria belongs to all of us and we must collectively safeguard its unity.

--GEJ, January 16, 2012.

As we commemorate the anniversary of the birth of the Holy Prophet Mohammed (SAW)...I urge all Nigerians to collectively reflect on the virtues and ideals which he exemplified and taught. The proper internalization of these virtues and ideals will undoubtedly benefit our nation immensely as we confront current security and developmental challenges. I sincerely believe that we will make much faster progress towards the realization of our shared vision of a strong, united and prosperous nation if more of our people imbibe the Prophet's lessons of peace, peaceful co-existence with others, tolerance, honesty, selflessness, sincerity, justice, equity and fairness to all. My administration greatly appreciates the untiring effort being made by our religious and traditional rulers to foster national unity and promote the peaceful coexistence of all Nigerians... and I urge them to do more in this regard. We shall continue to do all that we can .. to curb corruption, eliminate waste and redirect national resources to indentified high priority areas such as public infrastructure, power supply, transportation, agricultural development, education and other sectors that will have a direct and positive impact on wealth creation and employment generation.

--GEJ, February 6, 2012.

In taking the commitment of transparency to heart I gave my word to the Nigerian people that this administration would put in place policies, institutions and structures so as to ensure transparency in every sphere of our governance trajectory. I believe that the mandate

Nigerians gave to me following the election that was acclaimed by both local and international observers as well as a majority of the Nigerian people as free, fair and transparent is to do all within my constitutional powers for the good of our country. My dear friends on facebook, this administration has commenced a series of reforms in many areas including agriculture, power, energy, security, education among others and I want to specially request your support in prayers so as to ensure the success of these initiatives. Regardless of the orchestrated distraction, I will continue to place national interest above partisan politics for it is not about Goodluck Jonathan as an individual it is about Nigeria in the collective. It is not only about the present it is also very clearly, about our future too. I want to call on all those who may continue to view issues only from the prisms of partisan politics to take a break. Election campaigns are over, it is the season to deliver on good governance. In all the areas we have slated for reforms, we have, regardless of party, ideology or other interest, assembled and will continue to do so, very distinguished men and women of outstanding pedigree to carry out assignments in our nations interest. We must reward and call to service excellence and patriotism at all times.

--GEJ, February 10, 2012.

We are a people of great faith and the vast majority of our people are adherents of the world's major faith-based religions. My message to the nation therefore, as we celebrate one of Christianity's most holy days, is that we should continue to have faith in our collective ability to overcome all present challenges and take our rightful place in the comity of nations as a strong, united and prosperous country. As people of faith, we must never succumb to hopelessness and despair. We must rekindle and retain deep faith in our shared vision of greatness, and continuously renew our determination to achieve our immense potentials through total commitment and dedication to the fulfillment of our national aspirations...Nigeria will overcome its developmental challenges in the shortest possible time if we all resolve to set aside our differences, work together as one people, and foster peace, harmony and security in our country as requisite conditions for steady socio-economic growth and development. My administration will continue to give dynamic, purposeful and effective leadership towards the attainment of our goal of faster national progress and development. We shall continue to put the greatest effort into achieving a positive transformation in the lives of our people with the effective implementation of our agenda for national transformation. I shall continue to count on your support, cooperation and prayers for the progress and well-being of our dear nation.

--GEJ, April 7, 2012.

We have together demonstrated that the government of the people is an ideal that the people of Nigeria cherish. We have our differences as individuals and as politicians, but we have shown great faith in democracy and its institutions. We have refused to be limited by our differences. Despite reservations about some of our institutions, we have refused to submit to despair. This achievement is a testament to the courage and optimism of the Nigerian people.

--GEJ, May 29, 2012.

I pay tribute to all the men and women who have made our democratic experience meaningful: the ordinary people who resisted military rule, and have remained resolute in their embrace of democracy; the army of Nigerian voters who, at every election season, troop out in large numbers to exercise their right of franchise; the change agents in civil society who have remained ever watchful and vigilant.
I pay special tribute also to all patriots who are the pillars of our collective journey, most especially, our armed forces who have steadfastly subordinated themselves to civil authority... They have continued to demonstrate a great sense of professionalism. They have discharged their duties to the nation with honour and valour.

--GEJ, May 29, 2012.

Let us individually and collectively, continue to keep the spirit of this day alive. No task is more important. We must continue to do well as a people and as a democracy. We must remember where we are coming from, so we can appreciate how far we have travelled.. . We must not lose sight of those values that strengthen us as a people. ..I will do my utmost to continue to work hard in pursuit of the common good. There are challenges, yes, but we are working hard to address those challenges. And, by God's grace, we will succeed. My confidence is bolstered by the results which we have achieved in different sectors ..Our democracy is stable. Its foundation is strong and firm. Its future is bright.

--GEJ, May 29, 2012.

I had spoken about the policy of "one man one vote, one woman, one vote, one youth, one vote". I am glad to see that the Nigerian people in all elections have continued to respect the principle of fair play. Since this administration came into office, we have gone to great lengths to strengthen our democratic institutions, particularly the Independent National Electoral Commission. There are still persons who believe that elections should be violent and unhealthy, but they are in the minority. They will not derail our democracy because the majority of Nigerians will not allow them to do so.

--GEJ, May 29, 2012.

We cannot afford to treat the success we have recorded with our democratic experience with levity. Electoral reform is central to our administration's transformation agenda. I urge all political parties to embrace this reform... We will continue to work hard, to turn domestic successes into a source of motivation for greater achievements in the international arena. We are fully aware that it is only when our people are happy and confident that they would be in a good position to walk tall in relating with others.

--GEJ, May 29, 2012.

I want to talk about what we are doing and what we have done. I want to reassure you that we are making progress. But we can also do a lot more. We must. And we will. Our economic outlook is positive. ..In order to set Nigeria on a sound and sustainable path toward economic growth, this administration unveiled a set of priority policies, programmes, and projects encapsulated in the Transformation Agenda. These programmes and policies are aimed at consolidating our budget, fostering job creation, engendering private sector-led inclusive growth, and creating an enabling environment for businesses to thrive for the ultimate betterment of the lives of Nigerians. Today, progress has been made.

--GEJ, May 29, 2012.

The prosperity of Nigeria must start with improving the living standards of our farmers, and revitalizing rural economies across the nation. ..the appropriate infrastructure to support all-year round farming through irrigation is being rehabilitated and developed across the country. We must use our population to create markets for what we produce. We must grow local, buy local and eat local.

--GEJ, May 29, 2012.

It is our collective desire as Nigerians to improve the standard of education. We are particularly aggressive in addressing this challenge. As a former school teacher, I know that it is not enough to create jobs; we must develop human capacity, and train a generation of Nigerian children with better competencies and skills. This will grant them the edge that they require to compete in a skills-driven global economy, and by extension, strengthen our national competitiveness index. I want every Nigerian child to have an opportunity to receive quality education and acquire useful skills. We are reforming the education sector from basic to tertiary level.

--GEJ, May 29, 2012.

Globally, the role of women in governance has assumed great significance. In Nigeria, it is also widely acknowledged that women who constitute about half of the Nigerian population are great and invaluable assets, in both the public and private spheres. On our part, we have demonstrated serious commitment in further empowering women and projecting their role in public life.

--GEJ, May 29, 2012.

I wish to reassure every Nigerian that we will confront .. threat against our collective peace and security, and bring the perpetrators to justice. We will confront the few misguided persons who falsely believe, that through violence, they can impose their agenda of hate and division on this nation of good people. We must confront all those who think they can derail us by engaging in indiscriminate violence and mass murder, perpetrated in places of worship, in markets and public places, against the media, and security personnel. Nigeria is a nation of resilient people. We will never yield to the forces of darkness. Nigeria will never, ever, disintegrate.

--GEJ, May 29, 2012.

What matters most to all of us, is Nigeria. It is what binds us together. We have a duty to be loyal to our country. If we believe this to be a sacred obligation, it will not matter whether we are Christians or Muslims, or politicians, irrespective of political parties or divide. It really will not matter whether we are civil society agents, social activists or union leaders. What matters is Nigeria. This nation exists because we are one. We must, therefore, remain as one family, and work together to defend our country. Within .. years, it would be exactly .. years since the Northern and Southern protectorates were amalgamated and Nigeria was born. We need a lot more introspection, even as we look forward. We must take steps to heal the wounds of the past and work together, as a people with a shared destiny under one flag. We must strengthen our collective memory, draw strength from our history, and build bridges of unity to take our country to greater heights. This is what we should do. And we must. As a starting point, we must draw strength from our history and work to ensure that the labour of our heroes past is not in vain.

--GEJ, May 29, 2012.

Beloved countrymen and women . . our founding fathers brought joy and hope to the hearts of our people when they won independence for our great country. Nigeria made a clean break with more than six decades of colonial rule, and emerged as a truly independent nation. That turning point was a new beginning for our nation. Those who witnessed the lowering of the Union Jack and the emergence of the Green White Green flag continue to relish the memory, because that ceremony was not just about the destiny of a nation, but the future of a people. That future is here; we are the inheritors of a great legacy that goes even much farther into the past. The worthy patriots who made this possible were young men and women in their twenties and thirties. They worked together to restore dignity and honour to the Nigerian people. Their resolve united a multicultural and multilingual nation of diverse peoples, with more than 250 distinct languages and ethnic group. In 1960, our diversity became a source of strength, and the new leaders resolved to carry the flag of independence for the benefit of future generations. They had their differences, but they placed a greater premium on the need to come together to build a new nation .It is that resolve, and that glorious moment that we celebrate today. We also celebrate the patriotism of our heroes past. .who made the case for our independence...We remember as always, their contributions to the making of the Nigerian nation, and the efforts of their successors since 1960. We also celebrate the unfailing optimism and resilience of Nigerians who remain proud of our national identity.

--GEJ, October 1, 2012.

On this special day, I call on every Nigerian to remain steadfast, because our nation is indeed making progress. I call on every Nigerian to rediscover that special spirit that enables us to triumph over every adversity as a people: We weathered the storm of the civil war, we have refused to be broken by sectarian crises; we have remained a strong nation. I bring to you today, a message of renewed hope and faith in the immense possibilities that lie ahead. Fellow citizens, I have an unshaken belief in the future of our great Country. I consider it a priority and sacred duty to continue to strengthen the bond of unity that holds our nation together and to promote and nourish the creative energies of our people. This is a central objective of our administration's Transformation Agenda. Nigeria, I assure you, will continue to grow from strength to strength.

--GEJ, October 1, 2012.

.

We must continue to work together, confidently and faithfully, to ensure that our country's potentials are realised to the fullest; that our dreams are translated into reality; and that our goals are achieved. Let me reiterate that our administration is committed to the pursuit of fundamental objectives of an open society: the pursuit of freedom, security and prosperity for the Nigerian people, and the rule of law...Over the years, several leaders have built on the foundation laid by our Founding Fathers. The baton is now in our hands. Let me assure all Nigerians that we shall not fail. I am confident that Nigeria will continue to be a source of pride to its citizens; to Africa and the Black Race and to humanity; a land that is known for progress, freedom, peace and the promotion of human dignity. May God bless the Federal Republic of Nigeria. May God bless you all.

--GEJ, October 1, 2012.

If we must derive the optimum benefit inherent in our huge population, we must transform a higher proportion of this population from unskilled to skilled manpower. In truth, our population will not count for much if most of us are uneducated, unskilled and unproductive. Thus, to grow as a nation we must improve on the number of Nigerians that have access to good quality education at all levels.

--GEJ, October 7, 2012.

Today, in the face of critical resource constraints, the defining moment of our work is in actualizing our promises to Nigerians. We need to create a structured economy where everybody plays by the same rules, and contributes their fair bit. That is the Nigeria our heroes past craved for; that is the Nigeria we believe in; and that is the Nigeria we are building together.

--GEJ, October 10, 2012.

As we build this nation and walk the path of development, we must be mindful of the realities of our circumstances and those of the changing global economy... Fellow Nigerians, these are uncertain times in the world economy, and my Administration is taking necessary steps to mitigate possible adverse effects of the global economic slowdown on Nigeria. I assure you that we are going to build up the necessary savings to protect the economy against a possible global recession or a slow recovery.

--GEJ, October 10, 2012.

Yes, we have challenges, but also incredible opportunities. Ours is the task of transforming these opportunities into real, tangible outcomes which all our people can experience and call their own. We need the cooperation of everyone to make it work, to grow the economy, and to create jobs for our people. I continue to call on all Nigerians to act. Making Nigeria work begins with you and me.

--GEJ, October 10, 2012.

I want to assure Nigerians that the future of our nation is better than its past. We have had some challenges and together, we have either overcome them or are in the process of overcoming them. In our overcoming, we have bonded together and our understanding of our unique Nigerianness has grown...we must use this year to further define the type of future we want as a nation... so we must do everything to ensure that the coming new century must be a Nigerian century and for that to happen we must sow good seeds today.

--GEJ, January 1, 2013.

As a collective, we as Nigerians have an extensive history...The country has come a long way from 1914 achieving great feats in social, academic, political and economic spheres and though still confronted with issues and challenges not uncommon with a multi-cultural society, Nigeria is considered a significant player in the comity of nations. We owe it to ourselves, to past generations and to the future generations to tell our own story, the story of our experience, our challenges and most certainly, our strides within the continent and the world. We must do this. To ignore the significant milestones along the path to this date, will be to ignore the essence of our statehood – and most importantly, our most critical responsibility for the generations to whom we will entrust the management of our nation. We owe them a duty to renew their commitment to the vision which seeks to respond to every citizen's prayer that this land of ours will live up to her great potential and unite us more than it divides us.

--GEJ, February 4, 2013.

I am aware that many Nigerians still have mixed feelings about the amalgamation. What has come to light, for me, as I reflect on the history of the amalgamation, is not the mistakes that certain persons and groups dwell upon, but the God-inspired greatness of our country. The amalgamation created a unique entity in the world; a country that stretches from the Atlantic ocean to the Sahara desert: a beautiful country, a richly blessed people, who have turned out to be some of the most resourceful and innovative people in the world in all fields of human endeavor. What makes our country great is not the rich natural resources that we are blessed with, but our diversity and the inner strength that is reflected by the people at all times - in good times, in times of challenge; the beauty of our land, the purity of our souls, and the incandescence of our hopes. Most importantly, what makes us great is the unique collection of people that God has placed here – and every day, I see this through their cross cutting interactions and exchanges, their industry and their dedication to be the anchor of Nigerian nation-building and the carriers of Nigerian nationhood. Nigerians who left home for various reasons and who today make up the Nigerian Diaspora are making major contributions to the global community in various parts of the world where they are. They can be found as doctors, lawyers, scientists, engineers, ICT experts, administrators, professors and nurses, and various other callings. In all of these areas they show their Nigerian attributes of hard work, drive, resilience and success orientation. As they connect from the global to the local, they demonstrate the same Nigerianness and connect with the larger community of Nigerians at home.

--GEJ, February 4, 2013.

As we reflect on the fact of amalgamation, I am also immediately reminded of the victory against all odds that our football team the Super Eagles achieved yesterday; demonstrating that our pride in the national colours runs deep. In those tense moments, yesterday, no one called out or recalled the ethnic background of the player – local or Diaspora - that wore the green and white jersey. This is the Nigeria we have all worked to create and the Nigeria we should work hard to sustain.There is certainly no question that certain affirmative characteristics like drive, ambition, hard work, resilience, entrepreneurial spirit and organizational acumen are distinctive traits commonly found among Nigerians of all ethnic groups. These are partly inheritances from our evolved and distinguished ancient cultures and partly the results of our common interaction in contemporary Nigeria. I am convinced that the story of amalgamation contains many lessons for our benefit. In spite of our diversity, the founding fathers of our nation found cause to work together and promote a sense of unity. We have seen a country buffeted by domination, even a civil war, and other challenges, but 100 years later, it remains one country.

--GEJ, May 29, 2012.

The One Nigeria consciousness which has kept us together is what we must safeguard. The question we must devote time and effort to is: how do we build the foundations for the Nigeria we seek in the next 100 years? I urge all of us, as Nigerians to rededicated ourselves to a Nigeria where our abundant talents, ideas, competencies and values drive the change that will shape an emergent Africa in the new world. Our belief as a people as we prepare for the next 100 years, must be that the unity of Nigeria is indivisible, non-negotiable, sacred and sacrosanct. No one should insist on reversing history; those who seek a return to pre-1914 Nigeria only seek to diminish our collective heritage; we must remain the forward-looking people that we are.... the journey of our country since independence has been directed at a destination of unquestionable greatness. We have no choice but to continue to work hard at building a powerful, cohesive, inclusive and progressive country that will remain the pride of all Nigerians and the black race in general.

--GEJ, May 29, 2012.

We should encourage all those Nigerians from all walks of life who demonstrate boundless faith and hope in the country to continue their emotional and practical investments in the worthy and glorious Great Nigeria project.31. We shall sustain and advance our country's emergence as a politically powerful, socially stable and democratic society; a technologically advanced industrial economy, a prosperous and equitable society and a powerful player in the global system. On balance, despite all the challenges, we have recorded great strides in building and welding a new Nigeria... As we keep our hopes alive and let our passion for development burn we will build the Nigeria of our dreams. I believe that Nigeria is destined for greatness. I see a united, peaceful and prosperous nation in the horizon. This greater Nigeria, will make generations yet unborn very proud. To this greater Nigeria, we fully commit ourselves. Arise we shall, and prosper, we will.

--GEJ, February 4, 2013.

It is about creating jobs, creating wealth, and ensuring a strong safety net for those being left behind. This is an onerous task that requires the support of all Nigerians. We have laid a solid foundation for our international partners to come in and fully support our efforts through investments. I can assure you that my administration is firmly committed to the full implementation of this agenda. The ongoing reforms would not only help us attain our long term development objectives as a nation but also engender a better and more fulfilled life for all Nigerians and in doing so, help build our international image.

--GEJ, March 18, 2013.

Irrespective of our religion or faith, all holidays provide us with a fresh opportunity to establish stronger bonds with our family, friends and all those around us for more enduring, harmonious and beneficial relationships. As we celebrate this year's Easter therefore, I urge all Nigerians to rededicate themselves to living in peace and oneness with all members of their communities no matter their ethnicity, religious beliefs or places of origin. By now, it ought to be an accepted fact amongst us that our immense potential for greatness in the comity of nations derives in the main from our collective strength as a country of close to 170 million people and the acclaimed richness of our diverse human resources and natural endowments. It follows, therefore, that to successfully achieve our vision of becoming one of the most dominant nations on the global stage in the shortest possible time, we must stay together as a people and continue to effectively resist by all possible means, the evil machinations of global terrorists and their misguided domestic accomplices who seek to provoke turmoil, hatred and harmful divisions   among   us.

I assure all Nigerians that our security agencies, armed forces and I will continue to fully discharge our constitutional responsibilities for protecting the unity and territorial integrity of this country with all the powers and forces at our disposal.

--GEJ, March 30, 2013.

We must have peace, security and stability to effectively implement our agenda for national transformation in all parts of the country and we shall continue to work ceaselessly to re-establish the prerequisite conditions for nationwide progress and development.For your part, dear countrymen and women, I urge you to continue to exhibit restraint and understanding in the face of seeming provocations. Those who mindlessly and indiscriminately attack churches, schools, health workers, motor-parks, banks and ordinary road users must be seen as they truly are: the brainwashed pawns of international terrorism.They do not represent any true religion or section of the country and we must never play into their hands by succumbing to their nefarious ploys to incite religious, ethnic hatred and division among us.

--GEJ, March 30, 2013.

We have a duty to stand firm against those who threaten the sovereign integrity of the Nigerian state. Our will is strong, because our faith lies in the indivisibility of Nigeria. We call on the citizenry to co-operate...Nigerians are peace-loving people..sad events perpetrated by those who do not wish our nation well have not changed the essential character of our people. I want to reassure you all that those who are directly or indirectly encouraging any form of rebellion against the Nigerian state, and their collaborators; those insurgents and terrorists who take delight in killing our security operatives, whoever they may be, wherever they may go, we will hunt them down, we will fish them out, and we will bring them to justice. No matter what it takes, we will win this war against terror. I am convinced that with your support and prayers, we shall overcome these challenges and together, we will restore every part of our country to the path of peace, growth and development.

--GEJ, May 14, 2013.

Let me use this opportunity again to also reassure you, Muslim brothers, and indeed, the whole country that myself, the vice president and our team will do our best to reposition the country. Christians and Muslims are brothers and sisters and we must live together. Those who are predicting that this country will separate based on our frontlines as at the time of amalgamation by 2015, they will know that those predictions may not be true. Nigeria is a deeply religious people of Christians and Muslims.For us, we cannot imagine a Nigeria without Muslims and Christians. You can call it another name, but not Nigeria. So it is a blessing that this is one country that you have significant population of Muslims and Christians and this religious diversity will enhance our development because we can get across the whole world, wherever we go we are accepted. That helps us in so many ways. We are not even exploiting our diversity because of the myopic views of the elites about our situations My brothers and sisters, assalam alaiku...And for the world to move ahead and for Nigeria to move ahead, for us to develop first and foremost, there must be peace and security. Nobody will come and invest in an environment where you are not sure of your workers and investment. As a nation, for our children to get where we want them to be, we must create a very peaceful environment for them. So, they can develop mentally and be focused and use their brains in a manner that will bring economic changes to us. In Nigeria, we are very religious people and we believe in one Almighty God and we will continue to pray, God will see us through

--GEJ, August 8, 2013.

Even in these challenging times we must encourage the good news narrative to thrive so as to drown out the unacceptable negatives in the polity...I will not rest until all these reforms and good news have direct impact on the lives of our people at the grass roots level.

--GEJ, August 1, 2013.

This is just the beginning of greater things to come for our country and our continent. The foundation of planning which we laid at the inception of our administration is being strengthened for greater service delivery for our people.... We cannot relent... it is important that we keep our eyes on the ball: a holistic turn around... As we make progress in every sector of our economy... We must pay greater attention to education. .. "a nation does not become wealthy by what it has under the ground rather the wealth of nations are today measured by what is between the ears of her citizens". To the world I say, we have the most industrious humans on earth and we are ready for business. To fellow Nigerians, our collective work for change is not done. Lets us not be discouraged by the attempt to drag us into partisan politics when the urgent issue of the moment is governance.

--GEJ, September 23, 2013.

Through thick and thin, we have built this country together. Through triumphs and trials, we have developed a Nigerian identity in our own way. In truth, Nigeria is still a work in progress and we are challenged everyday to keep building in spite of the various obstacles that we face. Our strength has been in our diversity. If we look back over the years, we can say confidently that there is every reason to celebrate.

--GEJ, October 1, 2013.

I admit that these may not be the best of times for our nation. Our people are divided in many ways – ethnically, religiously, politically, and materially. I cannot hide from this reality. I cannot hide from my own responsibilities...Whatever the challenges that we may face, we have every reason to be proud of our national accomplishments; we have every reason to remain proud and optimistic. Our collective national journey has witnessed great watersheds, thanks to our spirit of endurance, perseverance and sacrifice. Getting the rest of the job done with determination and courage is just a matter of time. We are Nigerians, a nation of talented people, endowed with resources, potentials, and Divine Grace.

--GEJ, October 1, 2013.

In our journey to greatness as a nation, we have built an economy that is robust and erected enduring infrastructure and institutions of democracy. Our social system is now more inclusive, open and compassionate. We are waging a steady battle against poverty, unemployment, and corruption. Our sense of community, solidarity and shared expectation is strong and capable of withstanding the present social, economic and political challenges that still confront us...we have a duty as Nigerians; whatever may be our differences or prejudices, to always put Nigeria first.

--GEJ, October 1, 2013.

Our politics should be an art of patriotic labour and selfless service to the community, particularly by the political elite who are placed in positions of great trust and responsibility. Politics has its own high moral principles which abhor distracting and divisive rhetoric. As men and women in leadership, we must continually focus on service, duty, responsibility, and the next generation. Those who are elected to govern at all levels must focus on improving the lives of our people, not selfish ambition... Whether we are Muslims or Christians; rich or poor; from the North or the South; East or West; regardless of our political affiliations, this is the time for every one of us to be a statesman!

--GEJ, October 1, 2013.

My clarion call..is that we should begin to align our political utterances and conduct solely to the nobler passions that unite our people. Politicians do not make a nation; ordinary folks do. Our nation is made great by the big and small efforts of regular citizens. These are the teachers and men and women in academics who inculcate the knowledge and wisdom that transform into tomorrow's wealth; the traders and market women who tend to our everyday needs; the farmers whose labour feeds the nation; the artisans whose work ensures that our homesteads are well maintained; the doctors, pharmacists, nurses, accountants, bankers, engineers, and other professionals who add value to our lives; the sportsmen and women and those in the creative industry who bring honour and fame to our nation; And the men and women of our armed forces and security services who toil day and night so that you and I may live in a safe and secure nation.It is the individual and collective heroism of these regular folks that has placed our nation on the path of greatness. Politics and politicians sometimes distract the people and create unnecessary tension...our .. celebration is about the same people, the people of Nigeria: their industry, sense of mission and purpose, and their patience and perseverance as we navigate historical turns in our march towards prosperity and self-sufficiency... I salute the people of Nigeria.

--GEJ, October 1, 2013.

My Compatriots, history has proven that nations take time to evolve. We should rejoice in our democracy because it enables us to be united by our differences, not destroyed by them. And, there is no more crucial time for us to be united than now.The threats we face may be real and immediate. But we are not alone in this regard. It is a difficult season for much of the world: industrialized or developing; rich or poor. What matters are the lessons we learn, the wisdom we demonstrate, and the victory we snatch from the jaws of likely. defeat. And I tell you, more than anything else, there are lessons to learn, and every cause to be thankful.

--GEJ, October 1, 2013.

Fellow Nigerians, the spectre of extremism haunts every democracy in every corner of the globe. While we celebrate our independence and good fortune, our hearts must grieve for those who have lost loved ones in numerous terrorist activities around the world. Back home, I admit being overtaken by deep feelings of grief, whenever news reached me of the appalling atrocities in some of our States, especially the North Eastern part of our country... This act of barbarism is a demonstration of the extent to which evil forces will go to destabilize our nation. But I assure you, they will not succeed... Our Administration will not rest until every Nigerian is free from the oppression of terrorism. I reassure you that no cost will be spared, no idea will be ignored, and no resource will be left untapped in the quest to enable our people live without fear. On this day, I implore every Nigerian – wherever you are, whatever language you speak, whatever your religious persuasion, whichever Political Party you support -: let us join together to fight this evil of extremism.

--GEJ, October 1, 2013.

Fellow Nigerians, this is a time to pull together behind the national cause: the cause of our freedom, and our future. We must rekindle the spirit of Nigeria, to ensure that every democrat and every lover of peace in this great nation continues to live in a free, peaceful, and secure Nigeria. On my part, I re-dedicate myself completely to the service of this great country... I am pleased to affirm that, no matter the challenges we face, we are on the right path to greatness.

--GEJ, October 1, 2013.

I have been consistently mindful of the weight of public expectation to find solutions to the challenges that confront us because the mandate we have is a free and sacred one. In all that I have done, I have been guided by this sacred obligation, to work hard for the good of Nigeria and to make life better for Nigerians. I want to assure everyone that Nigeria, under my leadership, will not fail.

--GEJ, October 1, 2013.

I can reassure you that Nigeria's place on the world stage today is strong and safe, and it is certainly a place of dignity and respect. We must continue to build on this by remaining a nation and a people committed to ideals, the noblest humanitarian values, and the rule of law. Our Constitution is anchored ultimately on the idea of freedom and fundamental rights: freedom of expression; freedom from discrimination; freedom to vote and be voted for, and the right to human dignity. These are the core values of a true democracy. These are the values of which we must never lose sight.

--GEJ, October 1, 2013.

Fellow Nigerians, the past .. years have seen Nigeria evolve on an epic scale. Our progress since independence has not always been smooth. This is, after all, our Fourth Republic... That is progress and it proves that, our differences – real and imagined - notwithstanding, we are, in every sense, a united nation. This is no time for the harmful clutches of parochial sentiments and the politics of bitterness, impunity, arrogance and unhelpful indiscipline. We must stand as one, with absolute commitment and resolve to resist any force that threatens us and the sanctity of our union.

--GEJ, October 1, 2013.

I recognize that it is not easy to keep believing in the possibilities of our greatness when our faith is constantly challenged. But let me assure you that, if we do not despair, we shall reap the reward of our labour in due season. It is my prayer that, another .. years from now, our children and grand-children will look back on our effort and be thankful that we kept the faith.

--GEJ, October 1, 2013.

There is a view by some of our people that we do not need to sit together to dialogue over the socio-political challenges facing our country. .. I was one of those who exhibited scepticism on the need for another Conference or Dialogue... However, we are in a democracy, and in a democracy; elected leaders govern at the behest of the citizenry. As challenges emerge, season after season, leaders must respond with best available strategies to ensure that the ship of state remains undeterred in its voyage. Nations rise to the challenges that each epoch presents. It is imperative therefore, that in our march to nationhood, we have to be dynamic in our approach and response to the problems, even as we seek solutions to them. We cannot proffer yesterday's solutions to today's problems.

--GEJ, October 7, 2013.

Clearly, every dialogue adds something valuable to our evolving Nation. ..as we continue to strive to build a strong and virile Nation, especially in the midst of agitations and tensions, we cannot deny the fact that sitting down to talk is one right step in calming down tensions and channelling our grievances, misgivings and suggestions into more positive use for the good of our Country.

--GEJ, October 7, 2013.

The concept of participatory democracy is such that even after the people have given their representatives the mandate to make laws and act on their behalf, there is also a space for the governed to make further input into the political processes, without undermining the authority of the statutory bodies. Sovereignty continues to be with the people even as the people evolve strategies and tactics to strengthen its foundation for the benefit of successor generations. It is this sort of collaboration between the people and established institutions of government, that will allow for a robust outcome that leads to greater understanding and a more cohesive and inclusive Union. For me, there is no alternative to inclusivity, equity and justice in a modern democratic state.

--GEJ, October 7, 2013.

What we desire is what can work for the good of our people and country. The goal is to bequeath a better and a greater Nigeria to the present and the generation that is to come...We have wasted too much time and resources, bickering over sectional versions of what define reality. This is an open-ended luxury we can no longer afford. Let us move forward, with honest conviction and patriotic courage, to strengthen this Republic, and get it to work better and brighter, for all of us, to the glory of God.

--GEJ, October 7, 2013.

As we recalibrate our efforts, we must avoid the pitfalls of the past, and stay focused on achieving results...We must move deftly to discount time lost so far, for failure is not an option.

--GEJ, October 17, 2013.

In spite of the circumstances of the birth of our country in 1914 and the several challenges of Nation building, Nigerians have in the last..years demonstrated the belief that our diversity notwithstanding, we are a nation with great potentials. The task before us is to build a strong and united union. In the last few decades, there have been issues that have challenged our determination as a people brought together by God in this great land of promise...this administration stands for a stronger and more united Nigeria and shall do everything within its powers to practically pursue this noble goal...We cannot ignore such challenges; rather we must realistically address them.

--GEJ, December 18, 2013.

As our founding fathers did, we must appreciate that we are one large, diverse family, under God, and take steps to understand those variables that militate against our unity and aspirations to build a better society, and confront them with collective determination to move forward, thereby making our diversity, our source of strength.

--GEJ, December 18, 2013.

Our democracy is still young and for us to provide life's abundance for our people and play a noble role in world affairs, we must nurture and cultivate correct democratic values..dialogue offers this unique opportunity for us to deepen our democracy and strengthen our Nation, rather than to destroy or weaken our union...discussion process is for the benefit of the entire Nation. Every Nigerian, as individual or as a group, has an important role to play to ensure its success.

--GEJ, December 18, 2013.

I am fully aware of the responsibility of government for ensuring the security of the lives and property of citizens. My Administration is working assiduously to overcome .. national security challenges, the seeds of which were sown under previous administrations. There have been some setbacks; but certainly there have also been great successes in our efforts to overcome terrorism and insurgency. Those who continue to down-play our successes in this regard..appear to have conveniently forgotten the depths to which security in our country had plunged before now. At a stage, almost the entire North-East of Nigeria was under siege by insurgents... But my administration has since brought that very unacceptable situation under significant control...the first major case of kidnapping for ransom took place around 2006. And the Boko Haram crisis dates back to 2002. Goodluck Jonathan was not the President of the country then. Also, armed robbery started in this country immediately after the civil war and since then, it has been a problem to all succeeding governments.

--GEJ, December 20, 2013.

While, by the Grace of God Almighty, I am the first President from a minority group, I am never unmindful of the fact that I was elected leader of the whole of Nigeria and I have always acted in the best interest of all Nigerians...I am as committed to the unity of this country as any patriot can be and I have publicly declared on many occasions that no person who threatens other Nigerians or parts of the country is acting on my behalf.

--GEJ, December 20, 2013.

I relate with all Governors irrespective of political party affiliation... I clearly differ in this regard, because as the President of Nigeria, I believe it is my duty and responsibility to create a level playing field for all parties and all candidates...I am still of the considered opinion that it would have been best for us to do all that is necessary to refrain from heating up the polity.

--GEJ, December 20, 2013.

I have not, myself, ever claimed to be all-knowing or infallible, but I have never taken Nigeria or Nigerians for granted.. and I will continue to do my utmost to steer our ship of state towards the brighter future to which we all aspire.

--GEJ, December 20, 2013.

Let us all..resolve..to make the ideals of peace, harmony, tolerance, love and goodwill to all even more manifest in our interactions with others. It remains my sincere belief that no height of human accomplishment is beyond us as a nation, if we can overcome our differences, such as they are, and forge a binding national consensus to put the progress and well-being of the country above all other considerations...My Administration will continue to implement its Agenda for National Transformation in furtherance of its avowed commitment to improving the living conditions of all Nigerians.We will continue to count on the prayers, support and cooperation of all patriotic Nigerians in the coming year as we consolidate and build on our achievements in several sectors including national security, power supply, communications, transportation, health and education.

--GEJ, December 24, 2013.

Whatever challenges we may have faced, whatever storms we may have confronted and survived, Nigeria remains a truly blessed country, a country of gifted men and women who continue to distinguish themselves in all spheres of life, a country whose diversity remains a source of strength.

--GEJ, December 31, 2013.

The amalgamation of 1914 was certainly not a mistake but a blessing…we must resolve to continue to work together as one, united people, to make our country even greater. I assure you that our administration remains fully committed to the progressive development of our country and the consolidation of peace, unity and democratic governance in our fatherland. ..I am pleased to report that we have stayed focused on this goal.

--GEJ, December 31, 2013.

Fellow Compatriots, I have always believed that the single greatest thing we can do to ensure all Nigerians realize their potential and play a full part in our nation's future, is to invest in education. The education of our young people is a key priority for this Government. We take this responsibility very seriously and I urge all other stakeholders in the sector to recognize the national importance of their work, and to help advance the cause of education in our nation.

--GEJ, December 31, 2013.

Fellow Nigerians..there is still much work ahead. We are determined to sustain our strong macroeconomic fundamentals, to strengthen our domestic institutions, and to invest in priority sectors. These investments will create more jobs for our youth…Our administration believes that the cost of governance in the country is still too high and must be further reduced. We will also take additional steps to stem the tide of corruption and leakages…Fellow compatriots, the task of making our dear nation a much better place for present and future generations cannot be left to government alone. I therefore urge you all to be ready and willing to do more..to support the implementation of the Federal Government's Agenda for National Transformation in every possible way. Let us all therefore resolve..to place the higher interests of national unity, peace, stability and progress above all other considerations and work harder in our particular fields of human endeavour to contribute more significantly to the attainment of our collective aspirations. I urge all Nigerians, no matter their stations in life, to rededicate themselves to contributing meaningfully to further enrich our national heritage. The time for that re-dedication is now, not tomorrow.

--GEJ, December 31, 2013.

We have our challenges but there is significant progress. With your commitment, with your prayers for us as a nation, we will surely get to where we want to go. All what we need to do is to make sure that we continue to do things correctly. That is why I have always pleaded with my fellow politicians that yes we must play the politics but let us take the interest of the country more than our own individual interest. And as we continue to play the politics in that direction, leaders will come and go but the country will stay.
Luckily, we have a constitution that says that nobody will be a governor or president forever.

--GEJ, January 1, 2014.

As long as we consider the interest of our country, children, grandchildren and we begin to plan for the next generation instead of wasting all our energies to think about ourselves, before we get to next 100 years, the country will be better. Nigeria can even change in the next few years and things will be better for everybody...we will surely get our economy to continue to move in the right direction and in the direction we want it to move. We shall continue to work hard to make sure not just that the economy will be growing based on economic parameters and indices, but that jobs are available for our young men and women and that food is cheap in our markets for ordinary people to buy and eat. That is the commitment of government.

--GEJ, January 1, 2014.

Despite our challenges, all what we continue to request from you is your continuous prayers because we believe... that no matter what an individual think he is, if God doesn't want you to succeed in achieving anything, you will not. You will get so close to it but at the end of the day, you will not get it. And I believe God is with us, I believe God blessed this country...there is enormous respect for the country. People believe that Nigeria is a country that can continue to lead the continent of Africa. We have countries that are ahead of us in terms of the economy, in terms of technology but they still believe that Nigeria is the country that will lead this continent because they have seen the potential in our country.

--GEJ, January 1, 2014.

Fellow Nigerians, as you notice an upswing in political activities I want to assure you that not only will I focus on my sworn commitment of providing leadership for ALL Nigerians, I will also run and encourage others to run a national campaign devoid of sectionalism because leaders ought to unite not divide. Again, the only difference we should look for in Nigeria is between good and bad not North and South.

--GEJ.

You may have read in the papers some persons virulent attacks on my person, calling me a disloyal person. I would only urge you to objectively look at my past and the past of those making these allegations and let your conscience guide you. As I said, the only difference we need to make in Nigeria is between good and bad not North and South. .. I was loyal to my leader, the late great President Umaru Yar'adua. I am loyal to Nigeria, I don't claim to represent North, South or a Committee-I represent Nigeria. I am loyal to Nigeria's economy, I don't have accounts or property abroad, ALL my children live and school in Nigeria. I am loyal to my wife and friends. Can those who accuse me say the same?

--GEJ.

When you are a sectional leader you feel insulated from problems outside your region and can "laugh" at the downfall of others. Leaders must unite the disunited and inspire hope to the hopeless. When any part of Nigeria mourns, I mourn, when they rejoice, I rejoice. I'll laugh with you, not AT you. I'll be a shoulder to lean on when challenges come knocking.

--GEJ.

Some have made their choice. However, I urge the rest of us to prepare to answer whether we are Northerners, Southerners or Nigerians. My passport and yours says Federal Republic of Nigeria. When we recite the National Pledge, we affirm to Nigeria. I'm a

Nigerian candidate and I will not be tired of pledging to Nigeria my country to be faithful loyal and honest! North or South, East or West, Nigeria is the best.

GEJ.

Fellow Nigerians. I am aware we are facing a lot of challenges but be assured that as a nation working together we are up to the task of meeting those challenges. Remember each and everyone of us has a role to play in Building Up Nigeria into a bastion of hope for the black world. .. I urge us all to always think, speak and act well about Nigeria.

--GEJ.

I need to say this very clearly. I want your votes so I can emerge as President of the Federal Republic of Nigeria after the election, however, my ambition does not take priority over the life of even one Nigerian. There MUST be no violence in the .. elections! No one who means well for Nigeria will advocate violence under any pretence. I call on Nigerians to be discerning and shun any calls to violence.

--GEJ.

I have travelled the length and breadth of this great country called Nigeria and I have seen the yearning for good governance and development in the faces of ordinary Nigerians everywhere. But we cannot achieve these lofty goals without peace. So today I urge you to take time out of your busy schedule and get to know Nigerians other than those from your immediate locality. To work together we must know each other. When we know each other it will be difficult for anyone to turn us against each other. I urge you all to shun any call to violence under any guise. Let us make peace and grow as a nation TOGETHER.

--GEJ.

Remember, there are only two types of people in Nigeria and they are good or bad and not Northerners or Southerners. Judge people by their character which they have control over and not by their places of origin which they have no control over. God Almighty made us and placed us in the families and locality where we were born. To then discriminate based on place of origin is to question the wisdom of God. And the wisdom of God is beyond the wisdom of man.

--GEJ.

Your story is my story. I know where the shoe pinches from you because I have been there. I was not born with a silver spoon so I am not aloof and unfeeling about the things that you go through everyday.. Who better to empathise with you and take actions to alleviate your situation than somebody who knows instinctively what you are going through because of a shared experience?

--GEJ.

I may be President today by the grace of God, but my true life story is not far from yours. Have you gone to bed hungry? So have I. Have you trekked kilometres to go to school? So have I. Have you walked bare foot? So Have I. Have you soaked garri because you could not afford anything better? So did I. Are you "managing" your Youth Corper 'allowee'? So did I. We are Nigerians and there is no "impossibility" in our dictionary! If then we share so much in common and I got here by the grace of God and your mandate, what willl stop me from doing my best to change your condition and our collective destiny for the good of our country?

--GEJ.

Some say I rely on luck, but was it luck that got rid of fuel queues, revived our textile industries, rescued our banking sector, ensured total radar coverage for Nigeria, is reviving our rail infrastructure or expanded the economy by over 8% making Nigeria the 4th fastest growing economy in the world? Those are the result of hard work. Only hard work can make Nigeria work.

--GEJ.

Before my sojourn in politics, I had no house, account or property outside Nigeria and all my kids schooled in Nigeria. When I became President by the grace of God and the wish of Nigerians my story did not change. Everything remains the same. My political offices never altered my taste for things Nigerian. Till the day I die, Nigeria will be the centre of my world.

--GEJ.

I am optimistic that the issue of North/South dichotomy will gradually fade away; in the new Nigeria, we shall be talking about Nigeria, not ethnicity, or religion, we shall focus on the economy, infra-structural development, employment and security. This is my covenant with Nigerians; With God's help I promise I will not disappoint you.

--GEJ.

I urge Nigerians to shun violence during the elections tomorrow and at all times. You cannot gain any lasting advantage via violence. Look at my life, I have NEVER been involved in violence in my life, yet God and the good people of Nigeria have been kind to me. Love of God and your fellow man will get you much farther than violence will get you.

--GEJ.

I thank those patriotic Nigerians and friends of Nigeria who participated in this event and projected to the International Community that Nigeria has had free, fair & credible elections. Now that some of the elections are over, I need to repeat what I said during the campaigns-There are only two types of people in Nigeria-good or bad-not Northerners or Southerners. Let us work towards bringing out the good in us.

--GEJ.

I thank Nigerians for coming out to vote. Of major importance however, is peace. Very little can be done in an atmosphere of strife. There is need to allow the rule of law operate unhindered, to stop pointing fingers at each other and point instead in the direction of progress. We need to begin with the end in mind and start from our family, then our community and make peace and then peace will make progress.

--GEJ.

Steve Jobs was a citizen of the world. Two months ago on this page, I opined that his idea which became Apple Inc had proved that ideas are more valuable than natural resources seeing as Apple Inc at that time overtook ExxonMobil as the world's most valuable corporation. I believe there are many Steve Jobs amongst our youth who would help build our country and add value to human existence. ..

--GEJ.

Remember, there are only two types of people in Nigeria and they are good or bad and not Northerners or Southerners. Judge people by their character which they have control over and not by their places of origin which they have no control over. God Almighty made us and placed us in the families and locality where we were born. To then discriminate based on place of origin is to question the wisdom of God. And the wisdom of God is beyond the wisdom of man.

--GEJ.

I will hate to disappoint you, but I will hate even more to disappoint the nation. So let it be clear that the collective interest of the nation will always over ride any narrow interests.

--GEJ, inaugurating Ministers.

Moments like this offer us an opportunity for reflection and rejuvenation so that the labours of heroes past shall never truly be in vain .. as we enter the last lap of our four years mandate it is also a time for the reconsolidation of the original dream of our nations aspiration for justice, liberty and the enjoyment of fundamental freedom..

--GEJ, inaugurating Ministers.

In the light of recent experience in our country, with all humility, I salute the Nigeria people and its indomitable spirit of never give up. It is that spirit well identified as the nucleus of our unity and our citizenship , which our founding fathers labored to uphold that we must now defend with every strength in our breath...

--GEJ.

I implore you to always face the challenges ahead with courage and patriotism by thinking first of Nigeria and contributing your quota to its development.

--GEJ.

We must enshrine the best standards in our democratic practice, good governance, electoral reforms and adequate protection to ensure security of lives and property.

--GEJ.

We want to refocus Nigeria to make sure that basic infrastructure is provided, the environment is created for private investment, both within and direct foreign investment. So jobs will be created. That is my dream for Nigeria.

--GEJ.

As a responsible government, we have not only put several security measures in place to address this menace, we equally churned out policies and legislations aimed at starving off the activities of these criminally-minded few and regaining the confidence of our citizens and that of the international community.

--GEJ.

We must all centre our political campaigns around issues that touch on the lives of the Nigerian people and how to ensure that before our centennial, we join the front ranks of the most developed nations on earth. This surely is far more productive than engaging in calumny and diversionary arguments that overheat the atmosphere.

--GEJ.

It remains my sincere belief that no height of human accomplishment is beyond us as a nation if we can overcome our differences, such as they are, and forge a binding national consensus to put the progress and well-being of the country above all other considerations.

-Goodluck Jonathan.

Our greatest and earliest challenge as an independent nation was the most unfortunate civil war of 1967-1970. To the chagrin of detractors, however, the nation survived and even came out stronger, primarily because of the initial strong foundation bequeathed to us by our founding fathers. ..it is only natural that our nation should have her own share of hurdles to deal with. Luckily for us, we are not living in denial of these challenges. Rather, we have recognized them and, so doing, we have put ourselves at an advantage in confronting and overcoming them. Whatever structure, programmes or legislations Government succeeds in putting in place, nothing much will be achieved unless and until the citizenry firmly commits to positive value orientation. This is one critical duty that belongs to both the leaders and the followers…fifty years ago when we started out, very few nations and commentators believed with any conviction that we would celebrate this anniversary as a united entity.

— Goodluck Jonathan.

I take public perception seriously, because I believe that citizens always matter. Hence we must therefore strive to maintain public confidence at all times.

— Goodluck Jonathan.

No longer must we tolerate the triumph of centrifugal forces whose main agenda is to distract and defeat the march of our people to the summit of economic self-sufficiency and political maturity.

—Goodluck Jonathan.

As we advance towards the strengthening of our democracy and the institutions and systems of our federalism, ..we will from hence avoid undue politicking and promotion of needless friction in the polity... here to serve Nigeria and Nigerians.

—Goodluck Jonathan.

In the comfort of our offices, let us not forget that majority of our people live below the poverty line and that many of the things we take for granted are in fact the unfulfilled dreams of many of our country men, women and children.

—Goodluck Jonathan.

For our democracy to be virile it must be genuinely competitive and strictly rule- based.

— Goodluck Jonathan.

Patriotism, accountability and transparency must underpin all our work .We should remember that the public has a keen interest in what we do as public officials.

— Goodluck Jonathan.

I charge all security agencies in the country to be more dedicated and vigilant. As we all know, maintenance of internal peace and security are necessary conditions for development and the conduct of credible elections...the eyes of the whole world are on us.

— Goodluck Jonathan.

As a nation, we have had some internal security challenges: The situation in.., the Boko Haram crisis and..the communal clashes in Jos, while there may be a few challenges to be addressed, the pragmatic resolution of some of these crises certainly limited the wanton destruction of lives and properity.

— Goodluck Jonathan.

As we progress into the .. elections, we must continue to anticipate and reflect on these ideals and remember that as member of the armed forces, we will be judged by our roles and the actions of our men.

— **Goodluck Jonathan.**

In defending the peace today, we are faced with new challenges, as exemplified by the very many civil crises that plagued the nation of late. We must remember that some or the greatest dangers to our democracy and freedom are shrouded in the perils of ethnicity and religious intolerance. These evils threaten our very existence as one sovereign and indivisible nation. We are therefore, challenged to discourage such sentiments and encourage our men to see themselves as their brother's keepers.

— **Goodluck Jonathan.**

Education is central to the human capital development efforts of any nation. Government will remain responsible in the discharge of its statutory obligations and we will not abdicate our commitment to the teeming citizenry of this nation

— **Goodluck Jonathan.**

Every vote must count. We will tackle banditry, thuggery and violence, which marred our past elections, to ensure free, fair and credible elections.

— **Goodluck Jonathan.**

This is a patriotic call to service and the self must therefore take a back seat, these rare privileges must not be abused!.. to accomplish important tasks that will result in economic transformation that promotes social mobility and equity, governance initiatives that subordinates government for the people and relationships that promote national unity, peaceful co-existence and security.

— **Goodluck Jonathan.**

You must hit the ground running! Time is of fundamental essence and no distractions in our mission would be tolerated. I take public perception seriously, because I believe that citizens interest always matter. Hence we must therefore strive to maintain public confidence at all times.

— Goodluck Jonathan.

I call on clergymen and statesmen, who really own this country because this country belongs to our statemen, traditional rulers, religious leaders, our men, our women, our youth. Nigeria does not belong to any politician or group of politicians. So we continue to urge you to pray for this country.

-Goodluck Jonathan

We cannot continue to lament the condition of our country but fail to make a difference in our little corner when given the opportunity. It is the aggregate of our individual thoughts and efforts that determine the destiny of our beloved nation, Nigeria.

-- Goodluck Jonathan.

I believe we the politicians are not putting out the right utterances and I am very sure that those of you who mean well for this country are not happy with us. As a politician, you want people to elect you, to perform a responsibility. If you mean well for the country, the country is nobody's personal estate but you want to serve. If people want you to serve, you serve and if they say 'no', you leave.

-- Goodluck Jonathan, 25/12/2014.

I get embarrassed when we the politicians, maybe including me make provocative statements, statements that create division among Nigerians; statements that can set this country ablaze. I don't think that is what a leader should do, I don't think that is the kind of seed a leader should sow. ..Look at African countries and those who kill to take power, they never end well…If a politician wants to take power whether at the house of assembly level, at the House of Representatives or senate or governor or president, you don't sow seed of discord and enmity because of course, it will consume you.

-- Goodluck Jonathan, 25/12/2014.

As a nation, we know that if anybody who has the privilege of being a governor of a state after serving, he becomes a senior citizen of that state, it is your duty to assist in-coming government. If you happen to serve as the head of government or as a president of this country, in fact, at the national level, we have the highest authority called the council of state, the permanent members of the council of state are past presidents and past Chief Justice of the country. The idea is that they have vast experience in a number of things and they can bring their experiences to bear in terms of advising any president at anytime, that was why that body was created by the constitution. But if we abuse ourselves, kill ourselves to be in office, then who will finish serving and still want to attend the council of state meeting for somebody who probably abuse you through life, it is not possible.

-- Goodluck Jonathan, 25/12/2014.

For a politician to stand up..to say that if he fails to win election, he will form a parallel government. What makes him feel that he must win the election? Even me as a serving president, what makes me feel I must win the election, no matter what I think I am. Nigerians will decide who will govern them at the state level, or federal level, state assemblies or the National Assembly in terms of the federal constituencies and the senatorial districts. It is not you who is looking for the office to think that you are the best person to be there. Are you the most qualified person even by certificate? Are you telling me your certificate is larger than that of others or you even have more certificate ? It is the chance of the people and the will of God.

-- Goodluck Jonathan, 25/12/2014.

Under my watch as President, no Nigerian will ever be discriminated against on the basis of religion, ethnicity or social standing.

—Goodluck Jonathan, January 2, 2015.

I will like to say this, once again, to my fellow politicians and political leaders. None of our political ambitions is worth the blood of any of our countrymen, women and children. The improvement of their lives and living conditions ought to be our primary motive and the driving force of our quest for political power and leadership positions. Let us not promote sectionalism, disunity, intolerance, hate, falsehood or the malicious abuse of political opponents. Whatever we feel or seek, we must have a nation and a people before we can dream of political ambitions. Let us put the nation and the people first. Let us all conduct our electoral campaigns with the highest possible decorum and civility towards political opponents.

—**Goodluck Jonathan, January 1, 2015.**

As I have always maintained, none of the challenges before us is insurmountable. We must come together as a people and work with single-minded unity of purpose to overcome them. As we go into this New Year, I salute the indomitable and resilient spirit of our people in Nigeria and wherever they are in the world. Our spirit of enterprise and the doggedness to succeed amongst all odds has been our strength. Let us continue our march to the future, towards the attainment of our collective vision of a strong, united, prosperous and harmonious nation – a secure nation for us and for our coming generations. I want to assure you that the terrorists will not get away with their atrocities: they will not win; they will be routed.

—**Goodluck Jonathan, January 1, 2015.**

In my political life, I have never been driven by the love of power. Rather, I have gotten to where I am today by the power of love which is the power that fueled the unity that saw Nigeria become the largest economy in Africa and defeat the Ebola Virus Disease... I will not dictate to you. I will listen to you. It will not be a monologue. I will dialogue with you. My brothers and sisters, come and join me so we can chart our forward movement together.

—**Goodluck Jonathan, January 1, 2015.**

Some people want to still keep these children as shoe cleaners, we must lift them up. Our children should not be used as cannon folders. They should be allowed to move forward to be governors like us.

—**Goodluck Jonathan.**

Some people call themselves statesmen but they are NOT statesmen. They are just ordinary politicians. For you to be a statesman it is not because you have occupied a big office before but the question is:what are you bringing to bear? Are you building this country or are you a part of the people who tell lies to destroy this country, to create enmity and make people who ordinarily would have been living together, fight themselves? Are you planning to set the country ablaze because you did not get that particular thing you want? Hiding under some big names and creating a lot of problems in this country, making provocative statements in this country-statements that will set this country ablaze - and you tell me you are a senior citizen. You are NOT a senior citizen; you can never be. You are an ordinary motor park tout.

— **Goodluck Jonathan, January 7, 2015.**

Nigeria is a nation of resilient people. We will never yield to the forces of darkness. Nigeria will never, ever, disintegrate

- - Goodluck Jonathan.

We may not have overcome our challenges, but neither have our challenges overcome us

- - Goodluck Jonathan.

Being a Nigerian is a blessing [and] a great responsibility

-- Goodluck Jonathan.

Nigeria will disappoint those who are thinking that the country will disintegrate. Surely, we will overcome this tribulation. Those who think that this country will be divided into North, south East and West, or whatever, we will not.

—Goodluck Jonathan , April 20, 2014.

There is no criminal group, within or outside this country that can break this country. No criminal group will disintegrate this country. Boko haram will come and go. We have overcome various challenges, God willing, we will also overcome Boko Haram.

—Goodluck Jonathan , April 20, 2014.

Let no one, whether the leader or the led, the high or the low, a member of the ruling or the opposition do anything to torpedo the system. Let no one, whether on the altar of personal ambition or pretension to higher patriotic tendencies, do anything that can detonate the keg of gunpowder on which the nation is sitting. It is time for all concerned to spare a thought for the ordinary citizens who have yet to see their hopes, dreams and aspirations come to reality, within the general context of nationhood

--Mohammadu Buhari, 22 July 2014.

I have led this country and I have a record. We were not perfect, but we were effective; we solved problems, and we made Nigerians proud. We rebuilt industries; Nigerians queued up and treated one another with respect; Nigerians took pride in our reputation for discipline.

—Gen. Muhammadu Buhari, rtd.

This gift of life and dream is why I stay in the fight for justice, in the hope it will eventually bring the kind of government Nigeria truly deserves. This is what democracy means to me— freedom, opportunity and dignity for all Nigerians.

—Atiku Abubakar.

A major reason why Nigeria is not working is the way we have structured our country and governance, especially since the emergence of military rule in 1966. We can agree that the federal government is too big, too rich, and too strong relative to the federating states. We can agree that there is too much centralisation of resources and concentration of power at the federal level.Nigerians would not have been calling for a National Conference, sovereign or not, if we were meeting our people's basic needs, including food, shelter, education, security, energy, and transportation infrastructure, if we were putting the country on the right path and every segment of the country feels equitably treated. And we would unlikely see people describing as a mistake the amalgamation of the northern and southern parts of Nigeria 100 years ago.

--Atiku Abubakar.

Many of our challenges are governance issues which can be tackled by a serious government committed to uplifting our people. To me then, the National Conference should design a political and governmental system that empowers local authorities and gives them greater autonomy to address peculiar local issues, and enhances accountability, while contributing to the general good of the country. Such a robust federal system would reduce the tensions that are built into our current over-centralised system.

--Atiku Abubakar.

Although our regional arrangement in the First Republic was not perfect - and did have its tensions - it certainly made for more local autonomy and better quality governance than what we have today. Our current structure, which can best be described as "unitary federalism" (a contradiction in terms), was created under our military regimes in the context of rising ethnic tensions and violence, an unfortunate civil war and the sudden rise in revenues from crude oil rents...Therefore, fixing Nigeria, to me, will require reversing decades of over-centralisation of power and over-concentration of resources at the centre. That is, it requires federal retreat or a degree of retrenchment of the federal government.

--Atiku Abubakar.

It is up to Nigerians to judge because whoever wants to lead this country will have to subject himself to debate and communication with Nigerians. So, if Nigerians believe he has the qualities ..it is up to them.

--Atiku Abubakar.

Despite our challenges in the area of security, infrastructure, politics and economy, I am grateful to God for keeping us together as one. It is my hope that we all will face the future of our country with confidence and fervent hope, that God will grant us the better tomorrow we are working for.

—Atiku Abubakar.

Although we are yet to get to the level of our dreams, nobody can deny the fact that we have recorded some landmark achievements since the colonial masters left our shore…Besides the developments across the country, we now have skilled and qualified manpower in virtually all fields of human endeavour…all of us may not be good doctors, good lawyers, good writers or good engineers but we can all contribute our quota where we have comparative advantage to make our country a better place.

–Sen. David Mark.

We are genuinely worried about our country; across political, religious and ethnic boundaries, we're truly worried because some key aspects of our values and tradition have been lost. In the old national anthem, we said 'in brotherhood we stand.' Do we still stand in brotherhood today? We used to be our brothers' keepers. Are we still our brothers' keeper? The answer definitely is no. Instead, we do those things that hurt others now. We need to look inwards and begin to search our minds. The ball certainly is in our court as leaders to do what we should do to reverse the trend. We must shelve the attitude of seeking power at all costs. We do not need to get desperate about getting to the top. At any level we are, we must be ready to contribute our quotas. We have so much human resources in this country but we are losing them because everybody has gone out of the country to seek greener pastures. We must do something to get them back. We need to find out the percentage of graduate unemployment. More than six million have already applied for immigration positions for few hundred openings. Let there be employment for our graduates in this country.

-- Sen. David Mark.

We have come a long way as a people. We should see ourselves as one people, one nation, with a common destiny. We cannot be moving in the reverse order when other nations are going to the moon. We have always admitted that the challenges are enormous but we must realize that nobody is coming from the space to solve our problem for us.

—Sen. David Mark.

We must..continue to exhibit good character and extend hands of fellowship and build blocks of unity and understanding to all irrespective of our perceived differences.

—Alhaji Aminu Tambuwal.

We have no doubt faced challenges living up to the promises we held at independence; we have missed opportunities, but we are also over-coming our challenges. I call on all Nigerians to join the present crusade to reinvent and transform Nigeria and, in this wise, I urge hope, courage, perseverance, prayers, reconciliation, peaceful-coexistence, and patriotic fervor to build the Nigeria of our dreams as no one else would do that for us.

–Sen. Ike Ekweremadu.

Let us not despair in the face of daunting challenges even if.. we ought to have surpassed certain minimum expectations. Nigeria remains ours to build and we must continue to maintain hope and optimism.

–Hon. Emeka Ihedioha.

It could be nightmares for Nigeria to break up. I personally have strong faith in the unity of Nigeria, that our unity is invaluable. That unity cannot be violated, so I believe that all these prophecies by doomsday prophets that Nigeria will break up will fail. It is not the first time we are hearing all those prophecies, it has always been there. Nigeria survived a very brutal civil war; so I don't see any fundamental issues that will lead to the disintegration of Nigeria in spite of the wishes of the doomsday prophets. Nigeria will remain one strong and united country.

—Sen. Victor Ndoma-Egba.

But even in the best of marriages, there will be issues, the thing is, how are these issues resolved? And I believe that we have the capacity, especially with advent of democracy. We will in a very fundamental way, resolve the issues that confront this marriage. Some of those issues persist because in the many years of military rule, we did not confront them. An issues that would have been resolved sparely long ago, stays up to now because they were swept under the carpet. So, I believe that the issues are there but the unity of Nigeria, like I said, is invaluable. We have been there for . . years. So, I think that the unity or the amalgamation is for the benefit of not just Nigeria but Africa as a whole because that amalgamation has put Nigeria politically in a very unique position to play the roles it is playing in Africa. And the consequences of the break-up of Nigeria are too dire for the world to ignore.

—**Sen. Victor Ndoma-Egba.**

We should continue to negotiate and re-negotiate the terms of the union. You don't go into a union and . . years later, you are still operating under the original terms of that union. So, we hope to every now and then, re-negotiate the terms of staying together. Yes, we moved from four regions in 1963 to 37 states today, was it through a democratic process? Certainly, not. It was by military fiat. States were created; local governments were created by military fiat not through discussion, not through negotiation. And the amendments to structures have come with consequences. That is because they were created under the military regimes. We have not been able to sit down and deal with the consequences of very fundamental structural issues that arose during the times of the military. So, we need to deal with some of the consequences that arose during the military.

—**Sen. Victor Ndoma-Egba.**

We must not allow doomsday prediction about Nigeria to come true.. What is needed now is for stakeholders in the Nigerian project to give maximum support.

—**Sen. Francis Arthur Nzeribe.**

We are happy that God has given us the minority of this nation an opportunity to...the leaderhip...we have seen the transformation of Nigeria.

-**Sen. Barnabas Gemade.**

I am convinced of the potentials of the great people of Nigeria to work together to build a modern Nigeria, as we move unto the second half of a new century.

–Sen. Abubakar Bukola Saraki.

I will say that we have fared very well in so many areas…We are moving along with the times, we may be slow but definitely, we have moved quite fast and I think that is enough for a developing nation.

-Sen. Odion Ugbesia.

Let's look at it from maybe a more philosophical point of view. We have fared the very way we are. This is the way God wanted Nigeria to be, that is where we are today. So, we have no cause to regret what God has done. And since our amalgamation..years ago, I think we have done marvelously well.

-Sen. Odion Ugbesia.

I think we have done well whether you like it or not. But it is true that we have challenges but we will overcome those challenges. I have had cause to say severally that 50 years, 70 years and 100years in the life of a nation is small. We are still laying the foundation for growth, we are still laying foundation for solution to some of the challenges that we have, laying institutional foundation to deal with corruption, we are laying infrastructural foundation for infrastructural development. I think we should continue in the same commitment, with time I think we will overcome all these challenges and we will be proud that we are Nigerians.

-Sen. Odion Ugbesia.

I have always said that at every point in time, we should choose the banner of peace, banner of dialogue over any other options available to us and not the option of violence, not the option of demonstration. I think that is the path that I will recommend. That as leaders of this country—the political leaders, the religious leaders, academic leaders, and cultural leaders should sit down and discuss things that can bring us together and not these rabble rousers threatening fire and brimstone. That will not help issues; we must sit down and talk…You can call it anything, any kind of conference that will promote peace, any kind of dialogue, exercise that will promote peace, that will promote harmony. I am in support of it and that is what I am recommending.

-Sen. Odion Ugbesia.

Let's face it. If all successive administrations had been employing youths, employable youths, graduates and non-graduates; if they had been employing them, would this number have risen up to this level? That is to tell you it's a systemic failure, right from the beginning…But..who equally have members who had been leaders in the country, either as state governors or had occupied one prominent position or the other; if they had not been able to do these things before now, why would they pack the whole thing and put on the President..? … Why can't..wait? They said they are very formidable; they are strong. They only way political parties take over power from an existing government is through the ballot. It is not by inciting the public through spurious allegations. So, the..should wait and contest elections.

—Hon. Daniel Ofongo.

As I am concerned, every Nigeria, irrespective of their tribe or religion, has the right to contest for any elective position. Everybody has the right to vote and be voted for.

—Hon. Daniel Ofongo.

The past..years bore daunting challenges in our evolution as a nation. Our values, bonds, shared determination and cultural heritage were put on trial at different times in these past years. However, our resolve to reunite, harmonize our differences and actualize the Nigerian project has kept us focused and moving forward as a nation. Through these years, we have redefined the true meaning of unity in diversity and tested resilience. Let..our past weaknesses become our strength; our past failure translate into our successes.

—Jonah David Jang.

Our administration is committed to complementing the federal government efforts towards building an enviable Nigeria; and we accept the challenge of the time, knowing full well that we must strive to fulfill the purpose of being here at this point in the history.

–.Jonah Jang.

As far as we are concerned, the oil sector where our revenue comes from should also be where our major jobs should come from.. we as a people are not players in the oil industry, something must be thoroughly wrong.. country that has been producing crude oil for almost sixty years still imports petrol to run its vehicles, imports diesel to run its factories. It is amazing that the people whose backyard where these things are taken every day still live in absolute penury and nobody is worried.

— Chibuike Amaechi.

Nigeria is one country in spite of our varying cultures, religion and ethnic nationalities; and we can only succeed as a nation if we stand united.

–Chibuike Rotimi Amaechi.

The greatest source of unity in a country is the military and you have suffered enough to fight for the unity of this country. I will say to you, the Nigerian military; don't be involved in Nigerian politics. Nigeria is too complicated for the military to be involved in politics. In Nigeria, we have many tribes. I tell people, I'm not Ijaw, I'm Ikwerre. There are people who are Ijaw, there are Hausas, there are Yorubas, there are Isokos, there are Fulanis. We are too many. If the military gets involved in Nigerian politics, the consequence will be too much…we thank all of you for remaining neutral and God will bless you for that. In the same manner, we will enjoin the Nigerian Police Force to remain neutral because the consequence of taking sides will be too grievous. All of us .. must contribute to peace in Nigeria.

— Chibuike Amaechi.

I have a very faint idea of what the civil war looked like...My children do not have any idea whatsoever of what the civil war looked and I don't want them to have any idea at all and God will not allow us to get involved in such situation where they will have ideas.

— Chibuike Amaechi.

We must learn to accept ourselves regardless of our religion, the colour of our skin, or the language we speak. My aide-de-camp is a Bauchi man, from Azare; my chief security officer is from Kano State and my orderly is from Taraba— these are people who are always with me. In the task of rebuilding this nation, we must recognize the work of the media as well. This is also about rebuilding the media; it is the responsibilities of the media to preserve what they have helped build— democracy.

--Godswill Akpabio.

Nigeria bears great hope, not only for Nigerians, but for the whole of Africa. We cannot afford to fail, for this would be an abomination and a curse on the black race. The challenge before us is to commit ourselves to renewed zeal to riding this country of elements who soil our name and compromise our posterity and destiny. The government cannot do it alone, though we have committed and will continue to pump in resources into the world against insecurity until every bandit has no hiding place and every kidnapper has been napped…As we round off the first 50 years of our nationhood on the next long march to our nation's centenary, we must be determined to do things differently while hoping for a better result for our country. We must harbour the notion that great nation are not built on the quicksand of tribalism and intolerance, but on the foundation of hard work, peace and moral justice.

– Godswill Akpabio.

Despite the seeming challenges facing the nation, there is a lot to celebrate, as the country remains one indivisible entity despite having passed through many trials, including a civil war. While there is no doubt that the nation could have developed far better than it is now, I urge the good people of Nigeria to focus on the positives as the challenges facing the nation are surmountable…We should all focus, as Nigerians, on how we can make our meaningful contribution to the maintenance of the peace, unity and development of the nation. A way Nigerians can achieve this is by ensuring that people of questionable character are not elected into power. The people should, in their full freedom, use their ballot to either remove or vote in people of their choice into positions of power, people who will be accountable to them and who will be ready to move the nation forward as we move the nation forward as we seek to join the comity of progressive nations.

— Adams Oshiomhole.

And as a minority young man, I want to thank the majority parts in this country for appreciating the fact that the minority should also be given an opportunity for the unity and harmony of this county.

--Gabriel Suswam.

I urge all Nigerians to neither despair nor be deterred by the current challenges of nationhood but look to the future with hope for a united, peaceful and egalitarian society. These challenges are a passing phase which any nation must face at some point in their history

– Gabriel Suswam.

The nation has reasons to appreciate God in spite of the current challenges. With single-minded commitment, hard work and sincerity of purpose, we can make our country great.

–Ibikunle Amosun.

Politics is about democracy, politics is about service, politics is about negotiation… Nigeria is for all of us and we must all discuss, dialogue and negotiate… We believe in Nigeria. We believe in the agility of this country and for the new breed, the transformation must show that we are united.

-- Babangida Aliyu.

In our quest to build a virile and vibrant nation..leadership with character, a leadership with integrity and a leadership with high moral rectitude; a leadership that will lay solid foundation for the brightest future for this country—Nigeria..we should go beyond passive electioneering campaigns in which many parties do not have manifestoes or programmes, where some people get into offices unprepared and not knowing what to do, hence they go about haphazardly executing the programmes of other parties, creating wastages or encouraging corruption..especially for a nation in developmental transition and bogged with historical antecedents of marginalization and mutual suspicion between and amongst the different ethnic nationalities that constitute the Nigerian nation..it is time we paid serious attention to the quality of people who aspire to lead us in this country. We have to take our destinies into our hands through deliberate and strategic deployment of the variables needed to get the best leader for our country. We can't afford to lag behind any more.

—**Mu'azu Babangida Aliyu**.

We should begin planning even ahead of the next fifty years by institutionalizing policies that will guarantee a better, more prosperous and economically independent Nigeria. Indeed, such a roadmap should be the corner stone of our golden jubilee celebrations, while applauding the enormous sacrifices made by our founding fathers. Such plan should provide basis for continuity of policies and programmes of governance. The journey of the next 50 years should be focused on the maximum exploitation and exploration of our abundant economic potentials—agriculture, solid minerals, tourism, arts and culture and others, to lay the solid foundation for our sustainable economic development and advancement in the pursuit of our shared vision…

— **Babangida Aliyu**.

We are confident that the nation will emerge from this trying time stronger, more united and more prosperous. Nigeria will only attain lofty height if citizens are prepared to make sacrifice

– **Muazu Babangida Aliyu (for NSGF)**.

Indeed, our story on the independence path has not been doom and gloom only; it is also strewn with bright patches and shades of greatness. We have had sporting glories, a Nobel prize in literature, representation in the top universities in the world and a Nigerian got in the Forbes 100 top list. For the most part, we groan so much at the cup being three quarter empty that we forget it's also one quarter full.

–Rauf Aregbesola.

We must also take time to reflect on the state of the nation. The Nigerian project is a bold experience in nation-building. It is an experiment that has proved to be a challenging undertaking. But, for me, building Nigeria is an experiment that is well worth the attempt. At independence, on this day in 1960, Nigeria was a country full of high hopes, and good prospects, with its diverse people filled with aspirations. But somewhere along the line, we got it fundamentally wrong, with the consequences that, .. years on, we are still struggling to get the basics right. The country is faced with tough difficulties and mortals dangers on multiple fronts. Our efforts at nation-building are being affronted by manifold crises... and terrorism among other woes. These are undeniably serious setbacks to our development march, but they do not amount to any permanent incapacity for us not to move forward. Indeed, setbacks are necessary but temporary impediments along the path to progress.

– Rauf Aregbesola.

I remain convinced that the Nigerian project is a viable one. And I am optimistic that we may yet get it right as a country; and convert our much vaunted great potentials into actual benefits for our people. All we need is sound leadership and good governance.

–Rauf Aregbesola.

As someone in leadership position, I set my sight firmly on the promises the future holds and the opportunities that our great country can offer. My aspirations are for Nigeria to be able to overcome its development challenges, and to become one of the top 10 economies in the world in the shortest time possible. But we need to work towards achieving these goals. As a matter of urgency, we must shift our economic paradigm from sole dependence on oil towards productive diversification. Agriculture is a viable alternative here. We must develop our agriculture towards achieving food security. We must give primacy to food security. We must give primacy to food production as a strategic national imperative, for it is a sure basis for sustainable economic development.

–**Rauf Aregbesola.**

Our present chronic youth unemployment situation is a potential source of social explosion. There is profound wisdom in productively engaging our youths. Young people are some of society's greatest assets; but they can also be a major source of its problem. In Nigeria, youths constitute the bulk of our productive population, and that bulk is overwhelmingly unemployed! .. all we need do is to get our acts together; think and organize so that we can make the most of the opportunities available to us.

–**Rauf Aregbesola.**

I am not trying to make light of the formidable challenges involved in making a success of the Nigeria project; my point is that the difficulties are not an excuse for failure. In fact, they are a compelling reason for us to try to overcome them. It is in our utmost interest not to fail to try. Success is only born of trying, and I am in no doubt at all that if we genuinely keep trying, we shall surely overcome.

–**Rauf Aregbesola.**

Every year offers us the opportunity to review the journey of nationhood and to come to the awareness that just as we have the prospect of greatness, so also are we faced with the grim possibility of tipping over the brink; the probability of outcomes now depends on the choices that we make. It is my fervent hope and prayer, however, that we will always make the right choice and realize our greatest potential.

– **Rauf Aregbesola.**

The peaceful co-existence, the respect and tolerance we have for our diversity, the way we have used our diversity to create strength, to prosper our lives, are the ingredients that we need for continued nation-building and I urge all Nigerians, irrespective of faith, irrespective of ethnic origins to continue to live peacefull .., knowing that this is home and they are all welcomed to do that and respect each other's belief, respect each other's sensibility. In that tolerance, we can really harness the diversity that God has blessed us with to develop a better state and a much more prosperous nation.

-- **Babatunde Fashola.**

Looking back at all that we went through in the past year, perhaps, the time has come for us all to take an introspective look at ourselves in an attempt to get to the root of our problems and challenges. The truth of the matter is that, whether it is the downturn in the economy or our worsening security situation, the challenges are traceable to ourselves.

--**Babatunde Fashola.**

We have, as a result of myopic self and group interests, created an octopus that is threatening to devour our collective heritage. That octopus is embedded in the twin evils of ethnic and religious intolerance. Recently, I had the privilege of attending the command performance of Kakadu, the musical, and it reminded me of the Nigeria of the early post-independence era when it did not matter where you came from. It is a story that we all must imbibe in order to recreate that glorious era when we were all Nigerians, though tribe and tongue and religion may differ. It is set against the background of a newly independent Nigeria brimming with hope, dreams and expectations. So we have a reference base that hope, dreams and expectations must not be lost, we must resolve..to return to ourselves and give impetus to them. To do this successfully, we must begin to believe in Nigeria Project once more. We must start by defining for ourselves the kind of future that we want. It is only when we agree on this that we can unite our efforts towards recreating the Nigeria of our collective dreams and make it come true.

--**Babatunde Fashola.**

Looking back at all we went through in the past year, perhaps, the time has come for us all to take an introspective look at ourselves in an attempt to get to the root of our problems and challenges. The truth of the matter is that, whether it is the downturn in the economy or our worsening security situation, the challenges are traceable to ourselves.

— **Babatunde Fashola.**

If we have agreed that we want to live together as a nation where we have common values, that we all wish to hold dearly to our hearts, they must be clearly spelt out on equitable terms based on justice…We must see problems in any part of the country as national problems. If there is environmental degradation in the riverine areas where oil is being produced, every Nigerian must show concern because they deserve to live like other Nigerians; they deserve good roads, clean water, hospitals and schools.

– Abdulfatah Ahmed.

The celebration of anniversary for any country is a period of stock-taking and reflection for us in Nigeria, it is time to examine where we were, where we are today and the way forward in the realization of the dreams of our founding fathers of nurturing and sustenance of an economically viable, socially cohesive and politically transformed society. We have had our ups and downs but the challenges are enormous and the prospects attainable. However, as we march towards to the year.., it is our ardent hope that our dear country will achieve ultimate developments as one of the biggest economies of the world.

— Isa Yuguda.

We want security in this country … we want food in this country. We believe we have a lot of dams; we need dams not just for hydro power but also for agriculture.

--Isa Yuguda.

God in the book of faith says, "Let the best among you rule" the instruction didn't say you are black or white or Yoruba or Hausa or Itsekiri, It didn't say let the equitable amongst you rule. That is the type of leaders we should look for, not to be bogged down by issues.

-- Isa Yuguda.

It is a matter of this entire nation: from the north to the south from the east to the west … This is a day for us to unite again; to come together as one people and one nation with one destiny. It is a matter for all of us… I am urging all Nigerians to come together as one; in unity. Nigeria is for Nigeria and Nigerians. This is a new era.

-Shehu Shema.

Exactly..years ago..we took our destiny in our hands as an independent sovereign nation. It was a journey that bore great promise, supported by even greater determination and commitment on the part of our people, for a bright future...years on, in spite of all the odds, the dream has remained alive. We have overcome all forces of division and remained a waited and forward looking nation. Yes, the road has been bumpy and the journey difficult at times, but, as a people we have persevered and the reward is the current democratic dispensation we are enjoying in a united Nigeria. This, more than anything, reinforces our hope in our nation, and keeps the fire of nationalism burning in us.

–Danbaba D. Suntai.

For the past .. years, we have continued to co-exist as one people united by God within the confines of a sovereign and indivisible Nigeria. Ours has been a journey that is not devoid of challenges, but as men and women of uncommon resilience, we continue to brave the storm. To us there is no alternative to Nigeria. We must not allow the labour of our heroes past to go in vain. As we march into the golden era of our great nation, we urge all compatriots to join hands in disregard of whatever diversities in building a modern, industrialized nation. Luckily at this time, democracy has taken a firm root in our nation, while leaders at all levels are striving to implement various policies and programmes that would take us to the Promised Land. Nigeria is indeed on the right track to greatness.

–Alh. Mukhtar Ramalan Yero.

We salute all those who made much contribution towards the development of our great nation. As we celebrate this important milestone, I urge Nigerians to reflect deeply on how we have come this far. We should draw enduring lessons from our experiences in the past, with view to bridging those gaps that divide us, and strengthening those bonds that unite us as a people with common destiny. We.. believe, and strongly too, that Nigeria can be on the mountain top as she should be if we sincerely employ the tool of free, fair and credible elections to unlock those potentials that enhance selfless service and promote good governance in our search for happiness and national renewal. There is so much we can achieve. What we need is will and the right leadership in a democracy where the votes will be counted and the voter will matter.

–Dr Ogbonnaya Onu.

I have no reservation because I will prefer to be a citizen of Nigeria than to be a citizen of any enemy state. But, of course, this is something that is unconditional; Whatever differences we have, we can resolve. God that made Nigeria one didn't make a mistake because Nigeria represents the most populous and richest black nation on the face of the earth and that has a purpose.

–John Odigie Oyegun.

This is the beginning of the efforts to deliver the Nigeria of our dream. We need team work and.. a leader who is a team motivator and a man who believes in Nigeria.

-- Segun Oni.

True federalism is equality …it means a nation where all of us can become whatever we want to be.

- Gbenga Daniel.

We should now come together to fashion ways to translate the prospects into concrete reality for the benefit of our people. We must..ponder over the past ..years, do a sincere introspection of our polity as it concerns unfulfilled aspirations, shattered aspirations, shattered dreams, failed hopes, disappointments and endless expectations among other innumerable shortcomings. With this we can chart a better course for ourselves as a people and for the progress of our joint commonwealth. Nigeria is still work in progress and our destination is a united nation where every Nigerian is able to attain full potentials irrespective of religion, creed, political leaning and ethnic orientation.

— Gbenga Daniel.

I have written at several times..that there can never be justice and development in our dear nation so long as some persons are seen to be more equal than the others before the law. The constitution of Nigeria makes all of us equal before the law. No matter how highly placed a person maybe he or she should be made to face the law whenever there is an infringement of such law. In my assessment, I regret to state, it seems corruption is gradually being accepted as a norm in our society, going by the recklessness with which politicians and their cohorts carry themselves while in office. They conduct themselves in a most untoward manner by engaging in acts of profligacy and malfeasance. They do this with unbridled bravado and care no hoot about whether their actions place them on the wrong side of the law or not. Curiously, even existing legislations in the statutes are not enough to discourage their sleazy appetite to dip hands into the national coffers. Interestingly, the universal practice is to apply accountability, probity and transparency in governance as a way of ensuring that democracy dividends reach the people. This practice has assumed some religiosity in the developed countries, especially the United States—the bastion of democracy. It is for this reason that, ordinarily, it would have been expected that whoever seeks public office should do so with some degree of integrity, transparency and dignity. Regrettably, this is not the case in Nigeria, because of the tendency by public office seekers to compromise their positions by engaging in acts that question their fitness for such offices. It is painful to state, without equivocation, that corruption has contributed more adversely to the development of Nigeria over the years than any other social canker. In fact, it has reached such a level that it is capable of endangering our nascent democracy unless drastic steps are taken to curtail it...Those who understand the dynamics of our peculiar political life will agree that our politicians lack the maturity and altruism to govern without divesting their own interests, particularly when such interests would affect their political careers in any way at all. In spite of all the efforts at combating the menace, corruption has continued to flourish. The reasons for this sad development are very easy to locate. The first is the lack of seriousness on the part of our leaders to prosecute the war against corruption sincerely and selflessly. All they are interested in for now is to use it to settle political scores. They do this unabashedly and ignominiously, thereby bringing our nation's name into disrepute.

—Dr Orji Uzor Kalu.

There is every temptation to write off the past..years. There are people who have insisted that we have no reason to celebrate the..anniversary of our independence. They say we have nothing to show for it. Some have boldly declared that Nigeria is a failed nation...It is clear that it has not worked for anybody, including the authors of the unitary government; and it is unlikely to work in the future. The over concentration of power at the centre marginalizes many sections of the country; and to insist on this arrangement is to perpetuate the unworkability of the Nigeria project. Let those who cry that true federalism is to "tear this country apart" know that they are engaged in cheap blackmail. How can we expect that Abuja should decide what goes on with the lives of the people at Isiala Mbono (for example)?

— Ikedi Ohakim.

Everything we did in the last..years to outwit one another has not worked. We have rather outwitted ourselves. The first step we take as we step into the next ..years must be the right step. This 'House' called Nigeria has fallen and will not fail. We fought a bruising civil war; everybody said the House will fall with civil war. It did not. We came out of it teaching the world something about conflict resolution. Coup after coup, the experts forecast our end as a nation; but we emerged from the military aberration more determined to work on the democratic process. It is not yet perfect, but we are still on the democratic route. The annulment of the June 12 1993 presidential election put the nation on edge. The prophets of doom said we are finished...We showed the world that when ever we are challenged, we can still rise to the occasion...it will also come to pass that this prophesy of doom will fail. Nigeria will emerge from..elections still standing as a leading country in Africa...That we are not accepting our performance so far as good enough is evidence that improvement is possible and progress is within our reach if only we can do the right thing and turn to a new direction. The question is, Can we? Yes, we can! Are we ready? That is another question!

— **Ikedi Ohakim.**

Why should a headline of simple story of a declaration to contest be casted as ''Battle Line Drawn''?...I plead with the Nigeria media to be temperate in its choice of language, especially in times as volatile as election periods. Nigeria cannot afford to be in perpetual conflict with itself. The media must help us learn to listen to one another and understand one another.

—**Ikedi Ohakim.**

The character of our politics must change. More intellectuals and all those with moral suasion to inspire the youths of this country as role models must "invade" the political arena to flush out charlatans and failed yahoo-yahoo men who have reduced politics in Nigeria to be a hideout for wanted criminals. A political arena overrun by a band of rampaging deviants cannot sustain any debate based on issues.

—**Ikedi Ohakim.**

We do not have love or passion for our country. Every Nigerian wants Nigeria on his or her own terms… in such a case where every Nigerian manifests an obsessive "entitlement mentality", Nigeria becomes an orchard owned by nobody, where everybody harvests what he or she can, but nobody cares about cultivating the orchard. This is what we have over the years called the "national cake" syndrome. It is only a matter of time for there to be nothing to harvest from the orchard and no more cake to share.

—**Ikedi Ohakim.**

Our survival as one united and indivisible entity, despite all odds, is in itself a cause for celebration and a pointer to a brighter future for Nigeria.

–**Mohammad Danjuma Goje.**

We unanimously took a decision that after .. years of slow progress, Nigeria must dream greater dreams than ever before. We took the decision that we must take steps that will actualize the dreams of our fathers and the dreams of our youths of today; and we unanimously took a decision that the time is now to put men and women in good places to run our nation in the right way; and we took the decision that to lead Nigeria in this new march to greater Nigeria there is no other one who can do it than...gentlemen who have no baggage behind their shoulders; no prejudices of the past, no blunders, scandals...My brothers and sisters, the biggest problem that Nigeria has been having is frequent somersaulting of policies: one government comes and discontinue what it met...vote for a greater Nigeria!   -

--Segun Agagu.

Nigerians will have to find a way to do away with the present system of god fatherism—an archaic, corrupt practice in which individuals with lots of money and time to spare (many of them half-baked, poorly educated thugs) sponsor their chosen candidates and push them right through to the desired political position, bribing, threatening, and, on occasion, murdering any opposition in the process.

—Prof. Chinua Achebe.

Nigeria's story has not been, entirely, one long, unrelieved history of despair. Fifty years after independence Nigerians have begun to ask themselves the hard questions. How can the state of anarchy be reversed? What are the measures that can be taken to prevent corrupt candidates from recycling themselves into positions of leadership? Young Nigerians have often come to me desperately seeking solutions to several conundrums: How do we begin to solve these problem in Nigeria, where the structures are present but there is no accountability? Other pressing questions include: How does Nigeria bring all the human and material resources it has to bear on its development? How do we clean up the Niger Delta? What do we need to do to bring an end to organized ethnic bigotry? How can we place the necessary checks and balances in place that will reduce the decadence, corruption, and debauchery of past several decades? How can we ensure even and sustained development? And so forth...

—Prof. Chinua Achebe.

I foresee the Nigerian solution will come in stages. First we have to nurture and strengthen our democratic institutions—and strive for the freest and fairest elections possible. That will place the true candidates of the people in office. Under the rubric of a democracy, a free press can thrive and a strong justice system can flourish. The checks and balances we have spoken about and the laws needed to curb corruption will then naturally find a footing. A new patriotic consciousness has to be developed, not one based simply on the well-worn notion of the unity of Nigeria or faith in Nigeria often touted by our corrupt leaders, but one based on an awareness of the responsibility of leaders to the led—on the sacredness of their anointment to lead—and disseminated by civil society, schools, and intellectuals. It is from this kind of environment that a leader, humbled by the trust placed upon him by the people, will emerge, willing to use the power given to him for the good of the people.

—Prof. Chinua Achebe.

If the United states citizens decide to be bombing the USA everyday and ready to die, there is nothing Obama can do about it. The only thing he can do is to urge citizens to report bad people. If citizens refuse to report evil people then there is nothing anyone can do. Here in the USA in Chicago to be precise more than 10 people are killed everyday and that's the same thing. I am only worried that this is Abuja. There are people in power in certain parts of the country, leaders, who quite genuinely and authoritatively hate and cannot tolerate any religion outside their own. When you combine that with the ambitions of a number of people who believe they are divinely endowed to rule the country and who... believe that their religion is above whatever else binds the entire nation together, and somehow the power appears to slip from their hands, then they resort to the most extreme measures. Youths who have been indoctrinated right from infancy can be used, and who have been used, again and again to create mayhem in the country. Those who have created this faceless army have lost control

—Wole Soyinka, 2014.

We are saying that there should be peace in this country and there should be equity and justice. We realize that no one owns this country more than the other. Everybody is entitled to whatever he wants to be, the presidency is not zoned to any particular area. It is the right of every Nigerian to become the president of this country.. no one has the right to victimize any other Nigerian.

—Chief Edwin Clarke.

If it is government of the people, for the people by the people, opinions must be respected. Some people think that what they cannot achieve through due political and democratic process they can achieve by merely eliminating their political opponent, but they are wrong.

- Dr .Peter Akinda.

Since independence the country has never been so fortunate in having a visionary and well focused leader. Nigeria may rise again and sustain its avowed position as the giant of Africa, and its reputation as good people, great nation.

—Ayoade Segun.

We should not make this thing to look as if it is tribal, ethnic or regional. Some people are now saying that ..should not contest and power should remain in the ... I want to remind them that the..for.. years have been supportive to the political aspirations of the ...Thus, if today somebody from.. is in power, it is just like our own brother whose people have been very supportive of ours in the past.

-Alh. Muktar Shagari.

The country is in dire need of a purposeful and visionary leadership because the infrastructure in the country is in very serious decay, while there is need for the economy of the country to be given serious attention. It is time for politicians to start thinking more of Nigeria as a nation and stop all this tribal and ethnic politics. It is really important for Nigerians to choose a president that will turn the nation around and improve its infrastructure, security and power. These are the issues that should really worry Nigerians, rather than where the presidential candidate of a particular part comes from.

-Alh. Muktar Shagari.

Considering the enormous challenges and pains we have all faced as Nigerians, since our return to democratic rule in 1999, all Nigerians deserve special commendation for keeping faith with governments at all levels. It is indeed very amazing that Nigerians have been gallant in their resolve to see their great country, through to the Promised Land.

--Hon. Ikuforiji, fmr Speaker of Lagos State House.

We have a lopsided national structure. We will..discuss and resolve how we want to live together. The opposition in the country should get it right in order of priorities. Solving the Nigerian national structure is superior to the .. general elections you want to hold. We have had four different presidential elections in this country, of what use has the outcome been to Nigerians? What has been its positive effect on our people?. So, people like us believe that it is better to right the wrongs of our national structure than any .. general elections.

--Mr. Ayo Opadokun.

Our democracy depends its survival on fairness, equity and equality of treatment to the exercise of rights of all Nigerians without discrimination on any grounds whatsoever.

—Dr Peter Akinola.

I am on the stage in order to support …the man…aware that the country is undergoing political transformation and …will make sure that the labour of leaders past will not be in vain… the person we believe is sincere to address the issue of poverty in Nigeria;…to address infrastructure decay in Nigeria;… a man who will build bridge to ensure that Nigeria does not go back; it will continue to go forward ever.

-Amb. Isa Mohammed.

This is an opportunity for Nigeria to chart a new way forward. We have had ..years of independence largely governed by fear of one another. It is about time we came to the next .. years and chart a new course.

--Dr. Aliyu Umaru Modibbo.

I have a dream that despite all the upheavals, Nigeria will overcome. I have a dream that Nigeria will, by the grace of God be united, peaceful and prosperous. I have a dream that Nigerians will one day assemble and regard each other as brothers.

--Alh. Maitama Sule.

Well, to be honest, we have recorded a considerable achievement because if you compare Nigeria with other African countries, you will definitely acknowledge that we have made some progress. The only thing that we can say, without any equivocation, is that the extent of our progress is not as much as it should be. This was brought about by inconsistency in policy and leadership.

—Alh. Tanko Yakassai, Nationalist.

We thought independence would bring in joy and happiness, development, good quality of life and so on and so forth. Certainly, we are better than how we were at the time of independence because even from the point of view of tertiary education in the country ; at the time of independence, we only had University College, Ibadan. Today, we have over 90 universities, apart from other tertiary institutions, polytechnics and so on and the number of graduates they are churning out every year is enormous. So we are certainly better off than we were and particularly if you remember that the British came to take over Nigeria at the beginning of last century.

—Alh. Tanko Yakassai, Nationalist.

We were happy. We, who fought for independence, thought that independence would bring in virtually a solution to every problem in this country, but it is not so. It is not only here in Nigeria but in other parts of the colonial world. However, others realized, soon, that independence would not transform you into a better person without making your own efforts. One of our problems was the military intervention. It was a big setback for this country, which prevented the country from developing qualitative leadership. Secondly, the civil war set us back, because the consequences of the civil war are armed robbery, kidnapping and so on and so forth.

—Alh. Tanko Yakassai, Nationalist.

We have marched victoriously through the last 100 years, through all odds, to remain the greatest Black Country on earth today. Thanks to our founding fathers and all Nigerians, who have lived and still live through these 100 years. We must realize as a people that the years ahead of us hold greater glory for our country as we enter the next 100 years of our nationhood. It, therefore, calls for deep reflection and repositioning from all of us as individuals and, by extension, as a nation. Let us make the needed commitment by doing only what is right for the transformation of our country. If we all do this and maintain it, no nation will surpass our greatness by the time Nigeria is 200 years old.

--Mr. Mike Omeri, DG NOA.

Corruption breeds poor leadership, lack of accountability, marginalization, insecurity, social vices and neglect. Armed robbery, kidnapping, prostitution, cultism, ritual killing are by-products of corruption and the deterioration of the value system...When there is a weak centre and strong zones or states, the clamour to clinch the presidency by the various ethnic blocs will naturally die down.

--Chief Chukwuemeka Ezeife.

See what happened in Ethiopia, the country was lawless and fast disintegrating. But immediately they had a sovereign national conference; even those who wanted to separate changed their minds. Today, Ethiopia is a great nation and model of democracy. That is the picture we want for Nigeria. Public agencies have damaged the country. We need to find a way to cage them and put them in order. With that, the country will grow and nationals from other countries will come here and spend their money…If we really want to build Nigeria into a great nation…We need to have a roadmap, a broad spectrum of what we want. We ned to change our attitude to the country. We should offer solutions to the various problems and be involved in the bid to shape it up. That is when Nigeria will be ordered and structured for peace.

--Dr Federick Faseun, OPC Leader.

The problem of Nigeria is not our politics but the fact that we forget too soon. We feel the pain of our flagellation just at the time we are being floored. Afterward, we go about as if nothing has happened in our history. Today, Nigeria staggers under a weight of insurgency and terrorism that is very alien to our ethnic and national character. And we have some do-or-die politicians to thank for this. Insurgency and terrorism descended on Nigerians in the wake of the 2011 elections, after politicians of a particular coloration swore to make the country 'ungovernable' should they lose the polls. When Nigerians massively rejected these politicians at the polls, these bad losers made good their threats and unleashed the dogs of war through the North-Eastern part of the country. Since then, Nigeria has become one massive killing field with an internally-displaced population of over three million. Shall we cow before those who have brought this tragic and catastrophic atmosphere upon us and reward them with the presidency?

—Dr. Frederick Fasehun.

The refusal to run this nation along the line of true federalism has created inefficiency, corruption and derailed the vision of the founding fathers. The unity of the country must not be compromised, no matter the circumstances; we must do something about it... We are not united. It is also important to look at human rights, put a halt to impunity and corruption. Look at gender rights. Women are not fairly treated. There should be constitutional provisions on women empowerment, affirmative action for women, equal footing with men, even underage marriages. The only way to prevent break up is to allow the component units to determine the nature of their existence. We should be able to pull this country out of the woods. The danger of disintegration is real. It is clear and present everywhere. This..presents an opportunity to address it and prevent the country from breaking up.

--Yinka Odumakin, Afenifere Renewed Group Leader.

We have taken a long time blaming each other for every mistake. Nigerians should now peacefully discuss their problems at a round table. A national conference is apt when things are bad. Other countries also do it to review their progress and set agenda for the future. It should not threaten anybody. It is for the purpose of making progress. Other countries are working. Even countries less blessed than Nigeria. The socio-political and economic status should be reviewed. It should be reversed from enlightened self interest to public interest. It is because of self interest that we have hunger, disease, poverty, corruption and insecurity. The second thing I want..to examine is the dignity of the human person. This is important. History has proved this. During the colonial times, it was public interest first. During the first and second republics, the situation changed. It was during the second republic that we had for the first time, organized violence leading to loss of lives. Up till now, we have not gotten anyone convicted for organizing the riots. It was during the second republic that we had massive corruption. It was the beginning of this nation's collapse. Today, we have up to 20 million post-secondary graduates that are unemployed... Imagine the number of unemployed graduates ...Can the private sector handle that? The answer is no because it is also a by-product of the malaise of corruption.

--Alh. Balarabe Musa.

I am not working for government. I am working for Nigeria. For me, Nigeria is bigger than the government and anyone of us. There is nothing someone will do that everyone will agree with. there is nothing an individual will do that will bring about only positive comments. This is why when you decide to do something, it must be based on conviction. Once you have strong conviction about what you want to, you go ahead and do it. You shouldn't be bothered by negative comment.

--Prof. Chidi Odinkalu.

I understand that the major challenges we have is that our institutions are hardly functional. What we have are big men and no functional institutions. We have got to try to bring an end to era of big masters and big mistresses. So, working in human rights commission is an opportunity to help build an important institution. I am not saying I can rebuild an institution by myself, what I am saying is that I am willing to contribute to strengthening a national institution.

--Prof. Chidi Odinkalu.

Nigeria has space for good people, it has space for disagreeable people and it has space for the challenging people. What we need are institutions that mediate for all calibers of people. I am not God, so I cannot explain why we have different kinds of people in one country. In the same vein, I cannot play God by choosing who to work with or not to work with. Neither does anyone have the right to chose who he or she would rather work with. If I can work with anyone to make Nigeria work, then, no one should tell me how to comport myself. We should concern ourselves about delivering the aspiration of a shared country.

--Prof. Chidi Odinkalu.

I don't think that we are doing enough to protect the rights of anyone in Nigeria. The infrastructure of protection have been destroyed. When you look back in history, you will see that there was a time when things were different. If you look at the law report of those times, you will see that suspects were arrested. They were processed through to become accused persons and they were processed through to become convicts. If you also look at the prison records from those times, you will see that we had more convicts in jail than those awaiting trial. This so up until the late 80s... It was also the case that the police could investigate crime. The police had intelligent gathering mechanism. You had police intelligence officers in motor parks, universities, markets and other locations. These days, if a policeman is posted to these kinds of places, he will see it as punishment because he can't collect money. I am talking about the police because in any country, they are the first institution that protects the rights of people. If the police do not work efficiently, then we will continue to be in trouble. Nigeria police, as it is today, is largely privatized because of the large number of policemen serving private individuals.

--Prof. Chidi Odinkalu.

It is when you get out of Nigeria that you will appreciate the positive side of our country. You don't appreciate our value system or the confidence this country gives you until you leave outside. With the kind of education I got here, I was able to compete with just anyone from anywhere. In my time you could achieve anything you wanted to, partly because Nigeria was competitive. It might not be the case today in most schools. In my time, the best of a graduating class could compete with people from any part of the world. I have seen my former classmates doing well in different countries and maybe this is where the tragedy lies. We have exported too many of our best brains. Because of the situation in the country, I always tell my younger friends that they have got to be the best they can be. I tell them that today young people are competing with the whole world. Nigerian youths must work harder because those they are competing against come from countries that produce whatever they export (their products) in such large quantities. What they send to places like Nigeria is the excess of their large produce. In other words, Nigerian youths have lesser opportunities than my generation. The sad thing is that our leaders don't want to hear this message; neither do they want the younger generation to hear it.

--Prof. Chidi Odinkalu.

Unlike what we have in Nigeria, these schools you mentioned have good endowments. My school turned 35 last year and we don't have an endowment. The Nigerian Law School produced the current Attorney-General of the Federation and our senior judges, yet it doesn't have an endowment. There is something wrong with a system that doesn't compel someone like me who has been a lawyer for 25 years to give back to the younger ones. Despite this, you hear people complain about the fallen standard of education in the country. If we don't change how things are done in Nigeria, we will not be able to compete with the rest of the world. To be fair to government, Nigeria is the only country where people expect government to fund human capital development exclusively. A large amount of investment into human capital development should come from the voluntary and private contributions.

--Prof. Chidi Odinkalu.

For me, it was an ordinary experience. I had attended some of the best schools in the world right here in Nigeria. As unbelievable as I may sound, I am telling you the truth. I never doubted the fact that I competed against some of the best students in the world here in Nigeria. It has been an interesting experience teaching in Africa, Europe and North America. In terms of substantive content and awareness, we (Nigerians) know much better. But there is something we don't do well. We don't present our ideas coherently…Yes we talk a lot in Nigeria.

--Prof. Chidi Odinkalu.

The Nigeria civil war triggered my interest in protecting human rights….My earliest consciousness was after the war. I saw kids suffering. Death and deprivation were very real to me. I was lucky because my parents were teachers who also worked in the relief camps of Caritas International. But the seed of social justice was planted in me as a child because of what I witnessed.

--Prof. Chidi Odinkalu.

The way forward is that Nigeria must address..the national question that has been debilitating the nation. If the national conference is able to address certain issues, including the issue of federalism, how we are to structure ourselves, the power structure, state institutions, resource allocation, inter-governmental relation and the form and system of government, then this nation will move forward. We also need to prune down the size and cost of governance in the country. Nobody has told us what is being spent by ministries of government, nobody has told us how much is being spent by the National Assembly. We need to prune down the cost of governance. Also, the conference must look into best electoral processes that will produce effective leadership, not thugs that transmute into political leaders. Rule of law, good governance, accountability, check and balances, pragmatic limitations to the powers of government at all tiers must also top the agenda of the conference

---Professor Oyelowo Oyewo.

Are we really a nation or are we nothing more than a melting pot of squabbling and bickering ethnic and cultural incompatibles? Was Chief Obafemi Awolowo right when he described Nigeria as "not being a nation" but a mere "geographical expression"? These questions surely need to be answered.

--Femi Fani-Kayode.

Some of the questions that need to be answered are as follows- firstly is our union working? Secondly is our marriage a good one and if it is is it a happy one as well? Are we satisfied with what has essentially become a country that has been turned into nothing more than (with apologies to Chief Bode George) "Turn by Turn Nigeria?" where each ethnic group simply looks forward to enjoying its time to control the federation and all the nations resources from an all powerful centre? Are we not meant to be far more than this? Is this what the founding fathers of our nation envisaged?

—Femi Fani-Kayode.

The right thing and proper thing to do is to completely..attempt to find a presidential candidate that is a Nigerian before being a northerner, a southerner, a christian or a muslim.

—Femi Fani-Kayode.

Whichever way it goes and regardless of what we all think let us not allow this debate to be driven by the uninformed or ignorance, pettiness, hate and acrimony. Let us not insult one another or act as if any tribe or nationality are a collection of angels whilst others are nothing but demons. Let us join issues and exchange ideas in a civil, restrained and decent manner without hurling insults at one another or allowing our emotions to becloud our thinking.

At the end of the day we all want the same thing- namely, to put in place a system that is in the best interest of the Nigerian people and to empower a..leadership that will allow them to achieve their full potentials.

—**Femi Fani-Kayode.**

Chief Bola Ige once said that "the oil of the Niger Delta area acts as a glue that keeps Nigeria together". This is true. Yet the question that often comes to my mind is as follows- If the oil and gas had been situated in the core north, the west or the east would the major ethnic groups that hold sway in those areas have willingly shared it with the rest of Nigeria? Would they have remained in the federation?

—**Femi Fani-Kayode.**

Our priorities seem not to have been gotten right. The much-desired development looks slow in coming and presently, the gains that were recorded in the past are gradually ebbing. Our youths are not catered for, as the.. government has not put anything in place to cater for the welfare of the youths, with the attendant unemployment. If measures were put in place, the rate of crimes would have been reduced to the barest minimum, as most of the youths would have been gainfully engaged in one meaningful activity or the other.

— **Amb. Frank Ogbuewu.**

That we are still existing as one nation, despite our diversity and the odds against our dear country, are enough reasons to be celebrating, believing that God has great and special interest in Nigeria.

—**Hon. Bright Omokhodion.**

My advice is that we do not have any other country other than this. Look at the UK in terms of resources we are richer; our people who go there are forced to act in certain ways and it does not matter how big you are, you must respect the system … If we do things the way we do there, Nigeria will be better for it. Until we start having this reorientation and until this transformation wind…blows across the length and breadth of this country, gets to the right section we will make minimal progress, but I have very strong confidence in this country, because it is one that has come a long way…this country has been in the hands of charlatans, greedy men and never do wells for too long. If we stand up and say no to bad government, and to those who have track record of very funny characters. We will forge ahead. For the youths, I want to say the future of the country is in our hands. If we mortgage it, it will starve.

-**Prince Eka Williams.**

A lot of people have tried to attribute it to military rule but I will not want to blame the military alone for it…We tend to blame the leadership, yes, the leadership shares all the blame but the followership can't be exonerated. For instance if you want to join politics in Nigeria you must be very rich to enable you achieve result because politics has become an investment. If you have about N10m and you want to contest as a councilor you will be a fool if you get there and would not want to recoup your investment. I think it is our responsibility as followers to ensure that when people are campaigning for elections to know that we are not looking for just the immediate benefit in terms of what they give us to come out and vote. It is for us to vote individuals who we believe will not disappoint in office.

—**Muyiwa Akintude, Journalist.**

One of the ways we can get it right is to show commitment. It's always very easy to say that Nigeria is a bad country let me run away but those countries you are running to if they didn't believe in their countries would you have some where to run to? That is why Nigerians are humiliated even in their own country. If you go to the embassies for visa the way Nigerians are treated by fellow Nigerians who work as security personnel in the embassies is very demeaning and shameful. The first thing is to believe in our country and then take action, which doesn't need to be at the national level. It can be from your home or your little community. You have a councilor and your roads are in very deplorable condition and the public schools don't have the necessary facilities but there is a councilor representing that community, there is no reason that we cannot galvanize ourselves and ask that person some critical questions. If he doesn't meet our demand next time he comes to ask for our votes we should reject him. It may take a while but if we begin to do that a lot of things will begin to change.

—**Muyiwa Akintude, Journalist.**

I don't think it is the fault of leaders. It is the fault of the structure of government. Even most of the people who are making noise today, if you put them in government under the structure we have today, they are likely to be overwhelmed and listen to fraudsters, sycophants, and that are likely to make the same mistake because the system has given too much power to individuals, which is an invitation to chaos.

–Chief Alani Bankole.

We ought to pray for the peace of Nigeria; do not join anybody to cause trouble, confusion because you might bear the brunt. Some of you do not have international passports, but those asking you to cause trouble have passports, bank accounts and can vamoose at any time. Stay here and maintain peace because Nigeria will blossom. Whatever you get from the devil you will pay dearly. Refugees are not the happiest of people; don't make yourself a refugee.

—Most Revd Nicholas Okoh.

Our biggest concern, while we reflect on the condition of our country, must be how to bring about a fundamental change in attitude and a new orientation in Nigeria.

- Rev. William Okoye.

We must strive to make the fear of God and righteousness the foundation upon which this nation is built if we expect to see a turn-around in the fortunes of our beloved nation.

-Rev. William Okoye.

The task ahead for the present youth is huge. We are all witnesses to the corruption and lack of foresight of some of our present leaders. So we must be ready to redefine politics. We must be prepared for a change,… and the solutions lie on them, not the politician.

-Pastor Sam Adeyonju.

I want to remake Nigeria. The point is: Remake is a new thing, a fresh thing, a fresh hub, a chance for us to love ourselves to build a nation out of our own country.

-Mallam Nuhu Ribadu.

Nigeria is endowed with abundance investment opportunities in all the sectors, very receptive to investors, and some of its challenges are most often turned into opportunities by genuine investors, while the market is there for marketing of goods and services.

—Mustafa Bello.

We must keep hope alive. We are still together and would be together. There has been modest improvement and development. It could be better. But the atmosphere is not encouraging enough to hold those administrating the country accountable, talking about the security challenges. We must all return to the path of sanity to be able to develop.

–Pastor Ayo Oritsejafor, CAN.

I call on all Nigerian to..reflect on...integrity, love, compassion, humility and to pray for our leaders, representatives, the growth of the economy, the advancement of democracy and a violence-free nation.

—Pastor Ayo Oritsejafor.

If we want peace and prosperity then we must work for it and not lament over challenges; this is the spirit that will lead Nigeria to the promise land.

— Pastor Ayo Oritsejafor.

In 1960, the British colonial government relinquished the administration of Nigeria. On January 15, 1966, a military coup d'état ended the rule of the Nigerian leadership, which took over from the British. Corruption was the declared reason for the coup. This coup then led to a three-year civil war, 1967-1970...In effect..the civilian leadership were overthrown on charges of the same ineptness and corruption, which he had earlier decried and in the face of which he had called for an ethical revolution...the army seized power in order to put an end to the serious economic predicament and the crisis of confidence..afflicting our nation...added that..government would not operate kick backs, manipulated contracts or over-invoicing, nor would it condone forgery, fraud and embezzlement...Have we moved forward or backwards from this point.

—**Most Rev. Dr. Anthony J.V. Obinna.**

"I spent a lot of time thinking of Nigeria. My study was with a view to finding a modus vivendi for all Nigerians and I ended up with an ideology for Nigeria, which I called life enhancement. Enhancing the life of every Nigerian on the basis of equal value of every Nigerian. On the other side, I talked about one concept, live and let live. I found one concept to hold live and let live together, which is Convivial, the Convivial of the variety instead of the fittest. So, this is African democratic ideology, Convivialism.

—**Most Rev. Dr. Anthony J.V. Obinna.**

Can we live together as one people, one nation, in Nigeria? Can we, wit the multiplicity of our religions, of our ethnic groups, of our class structure, with the multiplicity of our conflicts, stick together as one country? I keep asking myself. Can we forge one nation, one national consciousness, through which every Nigerian, whether from Yoruba land, from Itsekiri, from Oyo or from Sokoto can live together?

—**Most Rev. Dr. Anthony J.V. Obinna.**

Right now, we are sitting on a keg of gun powder. We have known war. I was a prisoner of war at the end of the civil war. I was imprisoned in the military camp. So, I come from a background of having survived through the war and have been detained and escaped from prison. God allowed me to be alive till today...Do we have one God or many gods? This is part of the problem. If we have one God, we should have one humanity, one national family, but we have many gods, then we have multiple humanity.

—**Most Rev. Dr. Anthony J.V. Obinna.**

This is a very important issue at the apex level. So, the real issue for now is not PDP or APC, but our belonging together as one family, one nation, so that I can move freely from here (Owerri) to any part of the country, as I did in 1985, when I came back from the United States of America. At that time, I was able to travel through Nigeria without any harassment. But today, it is difficult to drive through Nigeria. It is unfortunate because Nigeria is such a lovely and a wonderful place.

—Most Rev. Dr. Anthony J.V. Obinna.

Whether it is the PDP or APC ruling the nation, our concern is how do we become fellow sons and daughters of God and respect and treat one another as such, without the feeling that you are inferior or that I am superior. This is part of my mission to equalize and or equilibrate the perfection of us Nigerians. We see each other not just as brothers and sisters but as sons and daughters, giving each person his due recognition as son and daughter. So, let everybody humble himself. Some people are suffering from a disease of pomposity, a form of psychosis.

—Most Rev. Dr. Anthony J.V. Obinna.

This is part of the predicament of Nigeria. If things had been better shaped, it would have been a different thing. Some of the countries that have had things better shaped are doing better. Even the small nations of Asia that were coming to us, including Malaysia that came to borrow palm fruits here, they are now super power in that area. Countries like Korea and Japan have become the Asian Tigers.

—Most Rev. Dr. Anthony J.V. Obinna.

Since this nation is multi- religious and multi-ethnic in nature and content it requires something that will hold everybody together. That has been my concern. If we start talking of Christianizing everybody, you create a problem. If anybody talks about Islamization, it will create problems. That's why there is a need for a certain transcendent that will guide whoever is at the apex of Nigeria...Efforts should be made to prevent sectarian apostles from manipulating either Islam or Christianity. Let us emphasize those things that are for the welfare of the people: education, health, electricity, because everybody needs these things, whether Muslim or Christian. If there is earthquake here, all of us, whether Christian or Muslim, will fall in. If there is an accident, all of us will go in. So, there is a certain humanistic strain. We shouldn't buy into Western secularization. Definitely, Muslims, Christians and Africanists, we agree on certain humanistic values. That was why it was easy to fight the issue of homosexuality and lesbianism. We don't tolerate those, whether as Africans, Muslims or Christians...But again, we have the danger of religious violence. It can come from Christians. It can come from Muslims. We need to eliminate it in our body politic.

—Most Rev. Dr. Anthony J.V. Obinna.

I am a Christian to the core but humanistic in my drives. As a lecturer for 17 years, the values I reeled out were life enhancement principles and they are neither Christian nor Muslim. This is from African Anthropology..life is supreme..God is the owner of life.

—Most Rev. Dr. Anthony J.V. Obinna.

The roles of Christians are living peaceably with all men and women and inviting divine visitation to overcome the evil forces that have held the country hostage in the recent past.

—Rt. Rev. Olusola Odedeji.

My assessment of Nigeria is that it is quite fair except that people have very negative thoughts; they have forgotten what Nigeria was like.. years ago.No matter the way you put it, Nigeria has gone a long way. It may not be as good as people think; they tend to compare us with countries like South Africa whose economy is owned 95 percent by white people and run by white people. Nigerian economy is solely indigenous. Nigeria is not doing so badly but I agree it can be a lot much better, but the major hiccup is the degree of corruption.

–Alhaji Lema Jibril.

As a people, we must depart from the old way of doing things and play by the rules. We have reached a level in this country where we must sanitise the polity. I am totally against any form of campaign of calumny and think it should be done away with.

–Sanusi Danfulani Sokoto.

Nigeria is a great country. We can make it even greater if we join hands together to harness the abundant human and material resources that we have been blessed with.

–Prof. Rufai Ahmed Alkali.

With the issue of ethnicity dominating the country's politics and presidential aspirants making heavy weather of the issue of zoning. Close watchers of the country's political arena hold the view that some of .. heroes of independence would be turning restlessly in their graves as they see the country they fought selflessly to acquire freedom for still tottering ...

–George Agba.

You would agree with me that historically, no president or head of state has been spared in terms of criticisms. Besides, nobody is against criticisms by the opposition, provided they are based on facts told for the purpose of enhancing good governance. But when what we keep hearing from the opposition are baseless and malicious criticisms, then you could readily agree with me that Nigerians are naively being misled with the kind of jungle politics which has its root in desperation and selfish interest.

I think people should continue to pray for Nigeria and for her peace as a country. People should not be engaged in proxy wars.

–Mallam Gidado Ibrahim (NAF).

Some.. elite..see..as not having the royal blood which should qualify him to rule the country. "Royal blood" in quotes here in the sense that they believe that to be qualified to rule this country, one must come from a rich background and have a root which could be traced to certain families of the ruling class. But God used.. to prove to them that a man from very poor background and with no political name can rule Nigeria. It is through.. that Nigerians started embracing the fact that, just like in the United States, anybody, irrespective of ethnic, social and class considerations, can rule Nigeria. So, I thank God.. who has stood firm behind.. despite all the political gimmicks being played to endorse sectional interest in the business of government... Our dream is to be the alternative voice for the.. where justice and fair play remain the guiding principles. I can tell you that our organization stands for justice and we will not rest on our oars to enthrone justice.

–Mallam Gidado Ibrahim (NAF).

I shudder. I worry for motherland, Nigeria. I wonder where the people's interests could be located in the postulations. Power or rather, the grabbing of political power, is all that seems to matter to the Nigerian politician. Except for a negligible few, service is far from the hearts of many of those fighting tooth and nail for offices. They seek to get power for self, not the collective; for enrichment, not empowerment. When service begins to count, we would not have people fighting the battles of their lives for offices. When elective offices stop to be the easiest route to instant wealth, you would find decorum and sobriety characterizing the chase for positions. Because, come to think of it, why would anyone maim and kill just because he desires to offer service? Why would anyone subvert the democratic process, rigging the poll, if all he desires is to truly offer service? Of course, we all know that pecuniary interests and influence peddling more than anything else fires the ambition for political offices here.

—Eric Osagie.

One of the ways to deal with the renewed upsurge in crime is the declaration of state of emergency in the job sector. Without jobs, the police can do little in tackling crimes. Many young men, who are graduates and are frustrated at their state of joblessness, are getting more desperate by the day. With their level of education and frustration, bullets don't easily scare them; the fear of death is not there. They are already dead without any means of livelihood, so what the heck if they die, trying to survive by hook or crook? That is the mark up of the new set of 'terrorists' we have now. Deadlier than Boko Haram. Lord, have mercy!

—Eric Osagie.

There is no place like home. The people back home are our blood and soul. Just because we live in a land that has constant water supply, electricity, hospitals, good roads and so on, does not mean we will forget out roots...Nigeria is our country... We want those who live in our communities, to live as we live here too. In all fairness..Nigeria is still young a nation. We can not compare it to the US, which is 234 years old. Still we believe that it's difficult to agree that Nigeria has justified the mandate of its founding fathers because we seem to be retrogressing in development instead of progressing. So the reason our dear country is still backward and unimpressive in growth is bad leadership, period! It is quite inconceivable that a country like Nigeria, full of great minds and gifted citizens has been governed by illiterates and bullies for so long. Umaru Yar'adua and Goodluck Jonathan are the first university educated people to govern this country after Zik in the First republic. It's appalling.

-Chukwuma Imo Oka (for Nzuko Edda, U.S.A).

Nigeria is a wonderful country. Today, it will seem as if tomorrow Nigeria will explode, but the next morning, Nigeria will be a smooth running nation, that is an asset to Nigeria. Our problem is that we have not got the right constitution. Either there is something wrong with the constitution or the operators of the constitution. There is too much power in the executive and there is too greed in the legislature. Unless we strike a balance between the excess power of the executive and the greed of the legislature, there will be continuous problem.

-Alhaji Shehu Kaikai.

You see, one of the oldest Soviet Republics, Kagistan, was having a crisis. They realized in the middle of the crisis that the problem was in their constitution. They went into the parliament and devolved some of the powers of the federation to the states. Now, they have some peace. We have seen two or three dangers in our constitution. We need to look at the constitution and then make people in authority more accountable. My concern with the constitution is that the non-elected people in the system have higher profile than those elected. Again, if people are honest enough, they would realize that all the cosmetic changes in the constitution are nothing. The real issue which they did not address is the devolution of power from the centre to the state and then if possible the equitable distribution of power between the executive and the legislature.

-Alhaji Shehu Kaikai.

In the end, the only enduring way to dispel bombs as a way of life in Nigeria and to stem the rising rates of robbery and kidnapping is to reinvigorate Nigeria with policies that will massively create jobs, humanize the Nigerian space – by providing sound healthcare, solid education and basic infrastructure – and demonstrate an awareness of what it truly means to be a leader. Leadership is not about throwing parties. It's not about buying new jets. It's not a matter of inviting a huge contingent of Nigerian politicians to enjoy a junket to New York, at the expense of the vast majority of Nigerians whose life expectancy totters at below fifty years. True leadership is about realizing the depth of the challenge facing one's nation, and then challenging yourself to rise to the challenge.

-Okey Ndibe.

Security tops the agenda. Some people do not want Nigeria to move forward. If Nigeria should move forward, it must have security.

-Hon Julius Asemota.

Yet we have been one Nigeria for 100 years. If we have not been in oneness, then, how have we survived this 100 years? The fact that we survived for 100 years as a nation called Nigeria means that there's some common bond. All we have to do is to reenergize that bond that has kept us together for 100 year, to make it better, not to destroy the little that is working.

-Air Commodore Dan Suleiman (rtd).

It's a unique year because it's a year of reflection. All of us should reflect this 100 years of Nigeria. We need to look at what has transpired. Is it the Nigeria of our dream? If not, why not? And when we know the why not, we need to look at the ways forward on how we can unravel the failings of Nigeria in order to bring a better Nigeria.

-Air Commodore Dan Suleiman (rtd).

The Nigeria of my dream is a united Nigeria, free of injustice, free of corruption, free of all the evils bedeviling this country today—insecurity, armed robbery, occultism, child molestation and all sorts of vices afflicting this country. And it is sad for those of us who mean well for this country.

-Air Commodore Dan Suleiman (rtd).

In Nigeria, it seems everybody has veered away from the ways of the Lord. Nigeria needs that spirit of repentance, firstly, we must acknowledge our failings. That's the essence of repentance. We must acknowledge that we have done wrong, that we have not followed the path of God. When we acknowledge these failings and accept our individual faults in not contributing to Nigeria and what Nigeria ought to be, we can recover.

-Air Commodore Dan Suleiman (rtd).

Nigerians should not only look at the negativities of issues. Let's find common grounds for things that we can develop to make this country great. All the elements that can make Nigeria great are there in this country. Why are we not exploiting it? It's because we are not working as one people. So, I think Nigerians should work toward a nation where everyone will have a sense of belonging. If we work as a nation like America, which has so many nationalities than Nigeria, yet everybody is proud to be an American, we will make it. America is progressing because they have common bonds and it's the number one nation in the world. So, our number should be our source of strength and not reason for our breaking-up.

-Air Commodore Dan Suleiman (rtd).

The Nigerian Army will fight till the last man to ensure the unity and territorial integrity of this country at all times..In particular, at this period that this nation is going through this insurgency problem, our last hope is on the army…Try as much as possible to make sure that Nigeria remains as a united nation, Nigerians must work hard to retain our peace…And those elements of destabilisation and destruction, we should fight hard to completely eliminate them

---Lt.-Gen. Azubuike Ihejirika.

For Nigeria, I think by age alone, we are matured enough to ask ourselves some questions and answer them in a truthful manner. We are just deceiving ourselves.

-Ms Ankio-Briggs.

I believe Nigeria can be a great country and that Nigerians can live together. Look at the circumstances we are in and we are still able to manage it and to drag it along. But we shouldn't be managing. We should have some rules and regulations that we all accept. We should agree on how and when we are going to do it and once we agree, it will be much easier. The problem we are having is that we didn't agree. And we have not found the basis on which we are agreeing. We must find that basis. Its possible to live together. But the question is how? What are the terms and conditions? Nobody is saying we shouldn't live together. We are saying how? Who brings what? Who owns what? Who controls what? How much should I bring? How much should you bring? How much? What if we keep everything and pay something to the centre? These are the things we need to look at together. We can live together, but how?

-Ms Ankio-Briggs.

For me, while I agree that when we look around the country, you are tempted to believe that there is nothing to write home about, there is no doubt that we have every reason to be grateful to God. The fact that we are still co-existing as a nation in spite of our differences is something to thank God for. When you consider the issues that have constituted major crisis in the nations around the world, which are small compared to what we have gone through as a nation, yet God, has kept us together, you will appreciate the fact that God has been faithful and good to us as a nation. When you consider all that God has endowed us with as a nation, I am a firm believer that God has a divine purpose for Nigeria...vices, like corruption that has held this nation down will be broken. Every believer should consciously live above board and ensure that you do not contribute to these vices in any way... The destiny of Nigeria is in our hands. What we do today, good or bad, will impact on the nation tomorrow either positively or negatively. It is time to put the past behind and re-strategize so that we can emerge from the ashes of corruption and decay and fulfill our God given destiny as a nation among the comity of nations.

— Bishop Dr. Mike Okonkwo.

We cannot afford to lose hope in this nation now because there is no doubt that God has kept us together as people for a definite purpose. Therefore, no matter the challenges we have gone through in the past years, we will rise up again to fulfill God's purpose for our lives.

— Bishop Dr. Mike Okonkwo.

We are yet to get a nation because we don't love ourselves. We are still living with ethnic sentiment. We still have divisions along ethnic and religion line. ..All along we have been after money, milking the resources God endowed us with... Nigeria breaking up is not in the interest of anybody as our strength is in our unity. But until Nigeria is led by selfless, focused leaders, godly leaders, statesmen and not politicians, we are not going to make any head way.

— Professor Tam David-West.

If we are still to remain together, there must be respect for the rule of law and justice, in a situation, where some ethnic groups would continue to oppress minority groups, there would be no choice than to stay apart.

— Chief Ritalori Ogbeboh.

It is better to be together than to go our separate ways. Nothing should be done by anybody to plunge this country into another civil war; no nation survives two civil wars anywhere in the whole world. What would happen to people involved in inter-ethnic marriages, we should always try to hammer more on what unites us than what can divide us.

—Dr. Fredrick Faseun.

I think every Nigerian agrees that there is load of benefits of being one country. All the negatives we hear is borne out of frustrations. But we all know that our place in Africa is derived from our size and population; we couldn't have got that without amalgamation. But quite a few believe and rightly too that they have been marginalized— but it isn't static, it takes different shades, we all get the short end of the sticks. But no Nigerian should be marginalized; we should be like the United States, where no one is marginalized.

— Barrister Tunde Odanye.

We have progressed from colony to an independent country, we have gone through a civil war and our educational system has improved from what it used to be during colonial times because today we have more schools in spite of the problems...Even though corruption has not been fully tackled, I think that we have improved because building a nation is not an easy task.

— Mike Ahamba (SAN).

We are possessed of what great nations require in order to become greater still. Our population is large, multicultural, imaginative, creative and adequately skilled. We have a large, diverse and fertile landmass. We have deep reservoirs of a wide range of valuable natural resources. We have plentiful water resources. We are a coastal nation. Above all we have our people: our population is large, multicultural, imaginative, creative and adequately skilled; we share a rich, varied and resonant history. There is much further to go but we have shown the power of our strength, our determination and our potential. We are Nigeria.

— Olaiya Philips etal, CEFONS.

Our politics however, is confrontational and dissembling. It undermines the morale and saps the strength of our people. Corruption is endemic. Large swathes of the country are under threat from militia and terrorist groups. What infrastructure we have is dilapidated. We do not have a maintenance culture. We have a battered and denuded education system. Our public health services are abysmal. From the national grid, we are unable to generate and supply power on a continue basis to any part of the country. Our armed forces and police are more feared than respected. Our social and political interfaces are one-dimensional: loud, louder and loudest. The truth is our people are not well served by our politics. Our people are hungry for a better politics; our politicians have to share that hunger for change – and be the change we seek. We are..years into a journey whose destiny and destination we are the current custodians of. We have endured and must endure further to correct the depth of our ailments. Nigeria can only rise to her God-given opportunities if we all dedicate and rededicate ourselves to building and edifying. This can only be attained if as individuals we abandon the glorification of self and uphold the common good of all, as preached and practiced by our Lord Jesus Christ.

— Olaiya Philips etal, CEFONS.

Rhetorics must give way to desirable perception to do good and take actions to atone for our past deceits and misguided leadership and corruption... years have come and will pass, and will again leave us with lots to reflect on. The lessons from the past..years should pilot us to avoid those human senseless errors brought about by in-ordinate ambition, greed, and selfishness. We should enthrone the spirit of selfless service to humanity, humbleness, honesty, integrity and humility to build a nation where the labours of our heroes past (that we also pray to become not the villains) shall not be in vain…We pray that we don't fail and thereby fulfill the prophecy of our detractors, wishing to add us to the heap of refuse of failed states or those wallowing in cesspool of stinking corruption and poverty! God help Nigeria to harness its abundant riches of natural resources and human potential…

-Maj-Gen I.B.M Haruna (rtd).

Beyond rhetorics, where is our dear Nigeria? The party politicians should answer with their manifesto, not with their generosity. Concealed in the philanthropy are the bribes that buy consciences to overlook corruption and flawed elections… Time is running out for us in Nigeria to be great people in the good sense, we have to put our act together and put aside the importance of our flowing gowns, chefs-hats, .. and the arrogant grand show of impunity and oratory-often put up to the detriment of the common people but as a mark of ethnicism. We should elect leaders that are honest, dedicated, and committed, to the common cause, of democracy, freedom and liberty within the law. We can pat ourselves on the back for having survived years of lost opportunities. We have failed to make good the vision and hopes of our nationalist leaders who held out the beacon of hope and led us to independence. We can congratulate our heroes past, but what about our generations…In our country, it is the dictate of the political leader's whims and caprices, of do-or-die and not empowerment programs…

—Maj-Gen I.B.M. Haruna (rtd), OFR.

We should courageously persuade our leaders to stop the wholesome abuse of power and abide by rule of law and due process. We should give no room for 'Nigerian factor', 'ethnic factor', 'regional factor', 'godfatherism ', where our moral standing as a nation is at stake. We should free ourselves of these negative labels for they are not the building blocks of our envisioned modern Nigeria…

We are not alone as a country with the experience of backwardness, poverty, discrimination, racism, illiteracy, denial of human rights, freedom and liberty within the law and equal before the law. The celebrated nations, big and small, had surmounted. Why not us? The USA and Asian Tigers are living examples of nations that have had to address their human development issues and have made their human and natural resources count towards their nation's power and influence. Why not us? Where has our abundant wealth counted? …If we had kept the peace elsewhere, why have we failed to engender the same peace and security in our nation stead? We need to find lasting solutions to Boko Haram, area boys syndrome, indigene-settler divisiveness, militancy, and we need to instill moral character

—Maj-Gen I.B.M. Haruna (rtd), OFR.

The past.. years have been rancorous and at times violent. The pre-independence era was more secure and we were making progress under the leadership of concerned dedicated and patriotic political leaders and elders…but..we have conveniently forgotten the essence of public service delivery to the people.

The model of a Nigerian, which is to be re-branded, is generally one of extravagance, arrogance, under suspicion of criminality, disposed to greed and primitive accumulation; inclined towards conspiracies to gather unmerited advantage on grounds of ethnicity, religion, or profession. All these inspire the subversion of our goals towards achieving national unity in diversity. We have to change our personal attitudes…We must change our attitudes so that we can be trusted and relied upon for better management of the human and natural resources with which we are greatly endowed….We had now become oil exporters and became rich and profligate, and even idle as we forgo our primary industry agriculture. Farming became a curse. Hunger and poverty became the lot for unemployment while the elite leaders bask in affluence...Military interventions denied us the growth of democracy and buried the state in the rubble heaps of dictatorship, corruption, indebtedness and generally moral decay in public offices and private life. This downward trend, caused by squandering of wealth, has diminished our promise of becoming Africa's and Black people's leader. Our political leaders who acted in no difference to check our moral slide did so as other African leaders of less populous and smaller countries and their dictators like Mobotu of the Zaire, etc. If we behave in similar immoral and exploitative manner we cannot be leaders of Africa or black people.

—Maj-Gen I.B.M. Haruna (rtd), OFR.

Many founding fathers would be disappointed...They would be entitled to feel that way, but the younger elements should resist that kind of appellation... Our leaders can honestly look back and take stock that can help recover what we have lost.

—Kalu Idika Kalu.

Let's tell ourselves the home truth. If you look at the career of people like Nnamdi Azikiwe, M.I. Okpara and Akanu Ibiam and take the totality of their perspective you see that they started envisaging a united Nigeria even some people go as far as blaming Zik that he was so intent on working for a united Nigeria that he didn't go the extra mile to take care of his own backyard. It is an unfortunate thing to say.There is nothing wrong with a united country. This is a strong country, if you can harness the energies of all these heterogeneous people. Indeed, he was going beyond Nigeria to talk about Africa. It's a wholesome thing to have that broad vision. You can say the same thing of Awolowo. Certainly, he was under a lot of pressure and he did cross the West to go Mid-West and South-South particularly. By and large, they went across their own spheres to seek support, likewise the Sardauna, who was even considered to be more insular. Even though Sardauna thought of getting the North to catch up with in whatever sense—educationally and otherwise with the South, he still tried to envision a united Nigeria. A lot of people are now appreciating his speeches. He was more of a statement, a national person than what was thought that he was, just a northerner.

—Kalu Idika Kalu.

Go to some of these countries, like cote d'Ivoire, until what happened to it and some other East African countries, they manage to maintain their schools, rail system and all the paraphernalia of development that were bequeathed them by the colonialists. By comparison, Nigeria still seems to loom large, in terms of order of magnitude of resources but certainly a country like Ghana has done relatively much better because they have been able to sustain their institution, they have not been experimenting the way we have. Immediately the British left, we started experimenting with all kinds of things-6334 system etc. We introduced the Nigeria Enterprise Promotion Decree and all kinds of people acquired enterprise that they could not run and that slowed down investment and meant that the growth of manufacturing couldn't continue the way it should have. If we had just modified and put our investment climate in order, so that those things would have been multiple of what they are, and the value-added components would have been much larger and the breath of industrial manufacturing would have been much but people wanted to grab a few of the things. Certainly, while some people were fighting, others were busy grabbing all these facilities. You can pinpoint precisely the fact that while we had all these advantages, the others that didn't have any advantage have a much more peaceful environment with which they grow than Nigeria. But you say that with a little bit of peace it is always easy to see that Nigeria can recover and move again and we are seeing some of them happening, even today, within the financial sector and communication sector etc. If we didn't have all these setback maybe we should be far ahead of where we are now. Malaysia came here and picked up palm oil seedlings and see what they have done with that and there is no reason we should not have replicated that. There is no reason we should not have massive fertilizer and petrochemical industries. There is no reason we should not have effective railway all over the place, as I tried to do when I was the minister of transport, to take the railway across the whole of the South from Lagos all the way to Calabar, extend it to Abuja and extend wider gauge all over the country that would facilitate the growth of agriculture and industry. It would have made a much more wholesome road network system without having to carry haulage on the road. The Volkswagen plant on Badagry Road, Ojo, was started the same time with the one in Brazil. The Brazil plant has since been producing 100 percent, but Nigeria's own has closed down you can see where our problems lie. The possibilities are there that if we can overcome them and recover some of our lost ground, indeed we will make much progress. We have not done as well as we ought to, in comparism with these countries. This is a time for us to honestly identify those grounds and try to put in place the appropriate policy and appropriate personnel that can help us overcome these difficulties.

—Kalu Idika Kalu.

You can ask what led to all these crises that necessitated a military coup. Earlier, I had talked about all the high hopes and expectations at independence. Perhaps, maybe there was greater struggle between the various component groups, maybe the resources were short of the grand expectation from independence and this engendered more struggle and this struggle could only be expressed through the political process in which people, from the East wanting more, people from the West wanting more and people from the North etc and therefore they began to see offices as institutions of ethnic nationalities rather than to Nigeria. The introduction of quota system has received some affirmative action because you can see a situation where you can say certain areas are not as developed, everybody should do in his own interest do something about it, special allocation, special training etc, but when you go beyond that to where it negates the growth of the entire polity then you can say that's when the rain started beating us, because we try to see national problem as ethnic problems and we started proffering ethnic solutions rather than national solutions to solve these problems. Then we were going away from the nationalism that we were all cheering when the Union Jack was coming down and the flag of Nigeria was going up. We were seeing a nation being born, but before we knew it we were now looking at nationalities emerging instead of the nation as a whole. We know the factors that led to the coup; the reception of the coup; the real interpretation of the coup and the subsequent negative events that took hold of the nation. If we can honestly isolate these factors out of these we can build much more lasting policies that can heal those wounds and Nigeria can now move forward to claiming the kind of position that the rest of the world really expect from her, given the resources available. When Congo and some other countries had crisis, Nigerian troops were sent there and they came back with accolades over how they comported themselves. They were disciplined and united. This gives you vision of what Nigeria upholds and with all the problems we have had. We continued to maintain that even during the Babangida administration. We introduced the Nigeria Technical Aids Corps, which we were using to extend hands of fellowship to other African countries. When I was in secondary school, Nigerian lawyers went to defend nationalists all over the continent. Nigerian personnel were active during the war. My father was part of the contingent that went to Burma, India, Ethiopia, and East Africa etc, they were there shoulder to shoulder with British officers.

—Kalu Idika Kalu.

We have to have hope…We must be honest to say this is the reason and this is how and this is the extent the rain has beaten us. There must be an honest return to merit. Merit is not to say that only the best will do, but there is an ordering that makes provision for different order of merit because they all provide for larger reinvestible surplus. As you put the good person to do his job, he can create more opening for others who may not be as good and you find out that those you may think are not okay may be the smartest ones, but if you didn't create the opportunities you will never give them a chance to prove themselves. We should create the real environment with which we can restore the real essence of merit to the system and we should apply this merit to community leadership; leadership at the local government, state level, federal level; leadership in business; leadership in business; leadership in various occupation and profession.

—Kalu Idika Kalu.

When you look back at what Nigeria should have achieved in terms of its great potentials, you feel not too excited... By now I think Nigeria should have been able to achieve quite a lot more if we had the right leadership all these years.

—Muyiwa Akintude, Journalist.

It is commitment to this country and a desire to see justice is done. We feel agitated whenever an injustice is inflicted. By our training, by our nature, by our upbringing we hate injustice; it is automatic that whenever there is, we will abhor it; we will fight it and also the burning desire to see the transformation of this country...this is the type of life I want to see in this country...This is what I am saying, I want the Talakawa to be employed, to be engaged in productive activities, creating wealth, taking care of their needs and not to depend on anybody but themselves...This is the type of situation I want to see in Nigeria.

–Chief Alani Bankole.

In Nigeria, governors are becoming more powerful than the people they are supposed to govern. Their security votes are only for their personal security. Meanwhile, these votes can comfortably guarantee the security of the people. Why don't we introduce a mechanism to reduce the security votes of governors and monitor their expenditures? What we have in Nigeria is what I prefer to call monarchical democracy. This is the type of democracy in which state power is exercised, without accountability to the people, by a privileged class of monarchs in the House of Representatives or Senate. It is the type of democracy we have in Nigeria, where those in government are exploiting the masses who they are supposed to protect. They are not faithful to the people. In Nigeria, we sacrifice national interest on the altar of self-interest... If Nigeria must move forward in the next two years, we must return to God and enthrone the practice of our core values in public life.

—Rev. Prof Emele Mba Uka.

The problem is that the political class is generally not patriotic. Look at the jumbo pay packets they have approved for themselves in the National Assembly. It is ridiculous and scandalous. They should slash their emoluments by at least 25 percent, in accordance with the intentions of erstwhile President Umar Musa Yar'Adua. What they are getting is out of proportion with the economy. Majority of those engaged in politics are there for what they can get from government and not what they can give to the nation. They are there to satisfy their personal interests. It is a shame.

—Rev. Prof Emele Mba Uka.

What we should be doing as a nation is to sustain the electoral reforms outlook of the Jonathan administration. The church has said it, and I here say it again that true democracy can be attained only when leaders are brought into political offices through an electoral process that is truly free, fair and transparent…As a step towards this attainment, political parties should consider, encourage and extol integrity, competence, fair play, service and complete adherence to party manifestoes over money politics and god-fatherism in their selection of candidates for elections.

—Rev. Prof Emele Mba Uka.

The issue of Christian-Muslim relationship in Nigeria is a delicate one, particularly, when we understand that whether you are a Christian or a Muslim, we are all the seeds of Abraham. The issue becomes a problem when we, as Christian and Muslim leaders, fail to fulfill our responsibilities of teaching our followers the proper things to do. It is the responsibility of religious leaders to teach their followers to observe the law and not take it into their hands, to promote shared values as contained in their Holy Books and not to extravagantly emphasise their differences. This is a sure way to promote religious tolerance and avoid the carnage that always follows ethno-religious crises that characterize parts of Northern Nigeria.

—Rev. Prof Emele Mba Uka.

I will say that we need a country, where justice, equity and fairness will reign. I want a country where no one will be oppressed. I want a country where people will respect agreement; we will see ourselves as one, irrespective of where we come from. We don't need a country, where people would be stopped from holding meeting because someone feels that they may take a decision that would not favour him politically.

–Dr Obinna Uzor.

I think we have not done very badly. It could have been worse. We had many attempts to subvert the democratic process but we managed to cling unto the tenets of the ballot box, power through the ballot box. Democracy is defined as the government of the people, by the people; what is more important and what is difficult is, for the people. It may be government by the people, yes, because you elect them; government of the people yes, government of Nigerians. Is this government for the people? Or for the wealthy? Or for the more educated class? What is the impact of government, or governmental actions on rural village dweller? Does he feel happier, or is he regretting that those in Abuja have totally forgotten him? This should be the yardstick to measure how successful democracy has been in our land. They are the people to speak; whether we have succeeded in our democracy effort or not, not the town dwellers who have light, water, roads, everything. But the rural dweller. How is he affected by the government action or inaction? If he feels happy, then you have succeeded. If he feels forlorn, dejected and rejected, then we have failed.

—Justice Chukwudifu Oputa.

Well, there have been a lot of improvements in the lives of the rural dwellers. When we were young, very few roads existed between villages. Now, there is no section of the country that is not connected with roads. When we were young, we had rail services, I don't know whether we still have them now. Then it took about four days to Lagos from Port Harcourt; two days from Port Harcourt to Kaduna junction and two days from Kaduna junction to Lagos. Till Ojukwu Transport started, and they could just go to Onitsha, sleep, early in the morning, you wake up and send the boy to cross into Asaba. Then Ojukwu Transport was about 6a.m and 6p.m. we were in Lagos. That was supposed to be an improvement, until the airlines came and did Lagos in about 45 minutes. We have really progressed.

It may not be as fast, but it is still progress from what we had in 1960 and what it is today. One area we may ask ourselves how far they have done well is the area of alleviating rural poverty.

—Justice Chukwudifu Oputa.

Nigeria is a potentially very rich country. If the resources, if the government and the people are well organized, to harness the numerous veritable mineral, human resources of this country, the talk about poverty will not be an issue at all. We have enough men and natural resources to give every Nigerian some comfortable measure of life.

—Justice Chukwudifu Oputa.

That depends on what part of the land you are. First of all, there was a time northerners thought it was a mistake. There was also a time southerners thought it was a mistake. But in 1960 everybody came together. If it were a mistake that Lugard made, isn't it within the capacity of man to correct mistakes? Our politicians should now engage in finding out why it was a mistake. What can we do about this situation we are in now—not one Nigeria? We can reverse that. That should be the starting point. Nobody wants Nigeria to be divided into North, South, East and West. No. This is the age of globalization. United Nations, African Union; this not the age we have to sort of divide ourselves into small, small nations. There is power in unity. United we stand. If Nigeria is a united country, with the population it has, with the natural resources, mineral resources it has, and if the population is well activated, then Nigeria will be one of the great nations.

—Justice Chukwudifu Oputa.

Religious leaders and the politicians should..endeavour not to abuse or use religion for political purpose. There is no Nigerian religion that doesn't believe in the existence of God. We all believe in one God. We may differ in how to approach that God, whether we call ourselves pagans or Christians each has a different approach... but the same God we are all hoping to meet one day. Whether you are a pagan, or a Muslim or a Christian, nobody has talked about any other God except God. So, if we all believe in one God, why should we be quarrelling? What's the quarrel about? Every politician needs religion when it suits him, to advance his political cause; when it doesn't suit him, withdraws into his shell. So, we should not allow people to deceive us. Religion brings us together; politics may divide us. And let us use religion for what it is meant for— to lead us to God.

—Justice Chukwudifu Oputa.

I think we have done a lot; we have progressed a lot. There was a time, Awolowo's time, the political-North for the North, South for the South, nobody talks about that now. We have realized that whether we like it or not, Nigeria has come to stay. We've also realized that Nigeria is now our fatherland. Awolowo, in 1948, called Nigeria a geographical expression. That there were no Nigerians as we have in this (country now). Well, that is not very true. Even in England, there was a time they had a division: Northern Ireland,

Irish, English, Welsh—there was a time they had friction. It took statesmanship of the leaders to emphasise what united them and to de-emphasise what divided them, and you now have the United Kingdom. They were not united before. The same thing can happen in Nigeria. Our leaders, if they want to create one Nigeria, what should be uppermost in their minds is to say things that will unite us, to do things that will unite us, not the opposite. God gave us a country and human resources… and you have to plan to have equity, so also you have to have a Nigeria of our dreams. It should be the task of the leaders, task of the teachers to do what they told them from youth about advantages of unity in Nigeria. It should be part of the curriculum of every school to teach Nigerian unity and the Nigerian anthem should be sung in every school every day. That should give you a sense of consciousness, then you are proud to be a Nigerian. And all our leaders who have made it, not those who are stealing our money, should be idolized, showcased. They should be told the type of leaders we want. Look at South Africa, when you mention Mandela, everybody stands up, and with pride…Let's make sure we don't miss the road by haggling over what is not important either to national destiny or to our own individual well-being.

—Justice Chukwudifu Oputa.

So, Nigeria wants to progress. We know where we come from; that is the 50 years; we know where we are tending to go, that's our future, if we know our past and know our present, then we can use a lesson from the past to influence our journey towards the future. And it will be a successful experiment.

—Justice Chukwudifu Oputa.

Democracy is government of the people, by the people, but the only argument is "for the people." If it's going to be for the people, your programme, your activities should be focused on the development of the people, not the only people in the town or city, the urban areas, rural areas, the villages.

—Justice Chukwudifu Oputa.

Nigeria is not homogenous, we are many nationalities called Nigeria, so many nationalities. An Igbo man thinks like an Igbo man; a Yoruba man should think like a Yoruba man, not like Igbo man. Is there anybody called a Nigerian? The answer is no. What effort are we making to create a Nigeria? As I said earlier, England, France, Germany, they all had this problem of creating one country out of heterogeneous mass of sectional interests.

—Justice Chukwudifu Oputa.

Yes, yes.. we need leaders with vision. Where am I leading my people? If Moses had no vision of New Israel, you think he would have left Egypt? You must have a vision. Where am I going? What do I need to reach where I am going? Leadership is a very difficult problem. And the country should be able to see from past experiences and also decide on the performances of those who want to lead them; whether this man is a better leader than that the other. But our sense is so circumscribed by tribal affiliations, tribal alliances..

—Justice Chukwudifu Oputa.

In one of my lectures, I dwelt on that issue and I thought it should be taught in schools. If a child is taught from class one to class six about the advantages of unity in the country, civics, he grows up with the idea that a united Nigeria is better. He grows up with, how do we get a united Nigeria? He is taught in the school. When he is 21 years old, his understanding has become very deep. But when he is young, between seven to nine years old, he doesn't understand what it means, gradually he agrees in Nigerian unity. Even in a village community, somebody from half mile away is a stranger. Maybe we need a good ruler to stress the importance of unity in diversity.

—Justice Chukwudifu Oputa.

I am going to ask a question, who elected the leader? The followers. You get what you elect, you get what you deserve. If you want a thief to be your leader, then you elect him; when he gets there to steal, you start to shout, what are you talking about? You know who he was before. A man who is dishonest cannot go there and become honest. He is from my own area. He is either a good man or a bad man; it doesn't matter where he comes from. And if you know that he's bad man, don't vote for him, because he's from your own area. And if you vote for him and he goes there and shows his true colour, don't complain. You knew that before.

—Justice Chukwudifu Oputa.

Corruption, as I usually tell them, is not an Igbo word or Nigerian word; it's an English word. Romans had it, too. It's not a peculiar Nigerian situation, it's a worldwide headache. How do you deal with corruption? If people know that one is corrupt, don't vote him into power. He will still be corrupt if he gets there. If he gives you money and you take it, you are also corrupt, whether giving or taking, its corruption. So when he goes there and steals, don't complain. You know who he was before you voted him— because he gave you money. The best way to stop this scourge of corruption is from the home. If the father and mother can tell the child, "Look at me, I have lived my life, I am your father, don't bring shame to this family. We struggled a lot to build the family name " … Once you steal and come and build your house in the village, you are a "big" man. It's a very big problem. Tackle it right from the home. The father and mother will have an idea of what is right and what is wrong, inculcating in them (children) this idea of right and wrong. Then the school should take over. Emphasise the good qualities of honesty, sincerity and then attack the bad things like corruption. Trust, no matter what, this cannot be easily bought, good name is more than pound or shilling, the costliest jewel of every life, you can take my pound... but if you take from me my good name you take that which does not enrich you but makes me poor indeed.

—Justice Chukwudifu Oputa.

A leader is somebody who should be what he says, what he does, what he wants; a good leader should inspire the people, and you don't inspire people when people know your background, know that they cant follow you. These things are there. At least, for the Igbo, they have very good respect for good name, not money. If you have money and your son is a thief, you will see the result. The good name is more that any precious stone.

—Justice Chukwudifu Oputa.

Whoever wins, let it be authentic, not fake. All we want is an election that truly reflects the voice of the people, which is the voice of God. We are just too tired of bedeviled and accursed elections. Enough is enough! For once, let's stamp our moral authority as Africa's giant. Let us be a giant for what is good and not what is bad!..We cannot afford to be fooled now or forever. We pray that like the New Jerusalem, a new Nigeria would emerge whose passport we would carry and not be ashamed.

–Mike Awoyinfa, Journalist.

In contrast, viewed at home and around the world as the sleeping giant of Africa, Nigeria remains the long-expected emerging power that has refused to emerge. ..all things being equal. Leading this country on the road to greatness may seem like a mission impossible but it isn't, all it takes is a leader who can stake all for the redemption of Nigeria. There are turning point decisions that have to be made to turn around the dwindling fortunes of this country that only patriotic leader with the grit of a revolutionary could make...

A leader aspiring to take Nigeria to the Promised Land must be willing to take such risk, if the need be, for the success of this country. Most of our leaders have always called for sacrifice from the people while they (leaders) live indulgent, opulent lifestyles. At the threshold of our centenary, there are things that matter now which must be done with all diligence and sincerity of purpose to pull this country out of the ditch.

—Rev. Chris Okotie.

When they say working materials, they are talking about money. That is high level of corruption. The highest corruption is for you to sell your votes for money. When you are talking about leadership, you are not looking at quality. You are looking at whether the person has money. That is the highest level of corruption and that is making it impossible for people who have knowledge, who have capacity, who are sincere, who are honest and they want to serve this country, they hardly ever get through because the voters put much emphasis on the money that politics then becomes something for the highest bidder. So, I cannot deny that there is no corruption in Nigeria. I believe there is corruption in Nigeria because even sometimes, you go to religious organizations, you go to Non-Governmental Organizations (NGOs), there are problems of poor management of funds sometimes.

—Labran Maku.

My brothers and sisters, these problems are not only in our nation...all over the world, we have problems of corruption, human trafficking, drug abuse not to talk of wars and fratricidal killings... We must not politicize the issue of security in this country…we will ensure that security challenges in Nigeria are overcome.

—John Cardinal Onaiyekan.

The government must ensure adequate funding of the operations of the security agencies. Government should improve on the area of intelligence gathering in order to ensure that crime prevention measures are adequately put in place. Perpetrators of these "high powered" crimes must be brought to book. Security operatives, who have waded through all dangers to save the lives of other Nigerians must be rewarded handsomely both with cash and the conferment of the national honours of valour…What is left for all Nigerians is to support our public office holders in making sure we achieve our goals as a nation. We must all make efforts to shun crime and resolve all grudges legally. We must learn to forgive one another and understand how to live with our differences and harness them to improve ourselves and our country.

—Jerry Chagga Makeri.

We must rededicate ourselves and work purposefully..so as to meet the dreams and aspirations for which our founding fathers made so much sacrifice. As a third year Harvard undergraduate in economics, we were told that three countries, Brazil, Nigeria and either Taiwan or South Korea, were at the same stage of economic development, and ready to take off on sustained economic growth and industrialization. Today, where is Nigeria and those other countries? While we have had some successes, I sincerely believe that we have had more failures than successes. Our founding fathers fought for independence so that we can have freedom and true democracy…Today, Nigeria is a byword for rigging and other electoral malpractices. In fact, we have failed so much our democracy that the military have intervened to rule Nigeria for about thirty years of our independence; and we have had civilians rule for about twenty years. Nigeria, in spite of the fact that God has given us abundant material and human resources is still a poor country. The ranks of the poor have greatly swollen since independence. The middle class has proportionately shrunk…to paraphrase our distinguished Nobel Laureate, Prof. Wole Soyinka, "talking to these people is like shouting to the deaf." Thus mediocrity rules the waves in a significant number of cases.

—Chief Chukwuma Bamidele Azikiwe.

The future is within our control, we should choose wisely in..elections. Let us realize that free and fair elections, by themselves don't deliver dividends of democracy. We may have free elections, the next challenge will be whether those we elected will deliver dividends of democracy or not…we wish to place emphasis on the fact that all hope is not lost if we use this moment correctly to evaluate our potentials and take decisive steps which nations seen today as great have treaded to become what they are. We are very confident that such conscious and deliberate plans could position us as a major player in the political economy of the world in the next fifty years. We believe that we are in the threshold of one of such historical moments—a moment to institute a sound democratic process; a process that is credible and committed to putting in power a leadership that derives its power from popular votes exercised in a free and fair election.

–Rev. Monsgr. Matthew Hassan Kukah.

I am not scared. We will do our job and ensure that we operate within the ambit of the law, whatever anyone says or threatens to do does not matter at all. I cannot be scared.

— Mrs. Farida Waziri, Fmr EFCC Boss.

What we have achieved very well in this country is digitalized corruption and crimes and because of corruption, crimes, tribalism and other negative vices that are eating up this country. That is why we as a nation at..cannot even manufacture a toothpick and that is a serious situation, because the toothpicks and other things we use in Nigeria are imported from china.

— Alhaji Abubakar Tsav.

Years in the life of a nation may be too short for any meaningful assessment of its volume, quality and pace of socio-economic and political development , yet it is worth celebrating for the express purpose of assessing progress against plans in order to effect correction and move forward. Nigeria has good reasons to fete over its..Anniversary, considering the peoples' settled committed to continue to inspire a nation which is socially diverse, economically empowered and politically active. In the period under review, Nigeria has been able to overcome its fault lines occasioned by the civil war and the annulment of elections conducted on 12th June, 1993.

—Anthony N.Z.Sani, Arewa Consultative Forum (ACF).

Nigeria as a nation has not been barren; our common union has produced a lot of things we can be proud of...We needed to focus on our strengths and not our lapses and then work on them.

—Mr. Dele Oye, ABUCCIMA.

There is no doubt that in spite of our numerous and seemingly insurmountable challenges, there is still cause for us to celebrate the attainment of..years of independence. Within this period, our beloved country witnessed tremendous progress and we must not allow the vision of our heroes to vanish. This is a period that calls for sober reflection and stock-taking with a view to repositioning Nigeria to face the emerging global challenges... It is worth mentioning that our country can only prosper if our people live in peace and harmony with one another notwithstanding our differences. In fact, our differences are the sources of our strength...avoid provocation and divisive utterances capable of derailing our hard earned democracy...be tolerant and exhibit high sense of responsibility and the spirit of sportsmanship in politics for our nascent democracy to flourish...avoid the politics of hatred and bitterness so that democracy would be meaningful to our people.
—Alh. Shehu M. Liberty, Borno State Government.

Exactly..years ago, the Union Jack bowed to the heroic struggles of our founding fathers. The green and white flag was hoisted to herald the birth of our great nation, Nigeria. Blessed with abundant human and material resources, it was certain that the Author of creation had especially destined our dear nation for greatness. A fledgling nation, in the hands of patriarchs, desirous to prove that the sacrifices of independence struggle was not in vain, the expectations and prospects of greatness were matched by the unwavering patriotism and determination to build one united, prosperous and democratic country. Nigeria towered! In Africa and in the global community, our nation became a colossus, a beacon of hope, the bulwark for the emancipation of the rest of Africa and the restoration of her glory and pride. Then, the unfortunate civil war. Then, the bitter lessons in the loss of love, in the neglect of our common fraternity. Then, the decades of military interregnum. Then, again the bitter lessons in the loss of the people as the sovereign, the travesty of the time, the aberration of the constitutional order, and the consequent anomie. Yet, against these odds, Nigeria emerged a united, strong democratic nation. The nation cannot undo her past for sure but she has since taken her fate in her hands. She has been reshaping the present so as to build a brighter future. We therefore jubilate that Nigerians are united in the indivisibility of their nationhood and in the irreversibility of democratic governance. We jubilate that despite teething challenges; we have advanced the vision of greatness and have taken concrete steps to build a prosperous nation far beyond where we broke from the tethers of imperialism. We jubilate that though the nation may not have met or surpassed the curve of soaring expectations, it has left significant mile stones. As we march into the next..years therefore..as the custodian of the mandate of the people shall continue to uphold tenaciously the principles of democracy and good governance, rule of law and respect for human dignity, the core ideals that makes us the choice of the people of Nigeria as well as connect our great party to the visions of the founding fathers. We urge all of us to join hands to harness the abundant resources with which the Almighty has blessed our nation. We wish to re-iterate our firm determination to rebuild a Nigeria which will be a pride to all mankind. We therefore must join hands to achieve this change. In this respect, we call on the political class and all those in positions of authority at all levels to draw a lesson from the selfless contributions of our independence leaders…we call on all politicians to reconnect to the ideals of our founding fathers in eschewing every tendency that can exacerbate the fissures in our diversity. We urge all those seeking for elective offices..to show maturity and restraint in their utterances and actions…imbibe the spirit of give and take as did our founding fathers so as to avoid any effrontery on the adhesive of national unity.

—Prof. Rufai Ahmed Alkali, PDP.

Nigeria's most important asset is its young people –more important than oil. History has proven young adults to be a powerful agent of beneficial change, especially if they are healthy and educated, with decent job prospects…With the right policies..Nigeria could easily become one of the world's leading economies.

—Olusegun Adeniyi, Former Presidential SA.

If there is a time in our National history when we must rise up together, and rebuild Nigeria of our collective dream, that hour is now. We have come to a point in our national pilgrimage, where we can no longer afford to waste further time in engaging ourselves in fighting unnecessary or unfruitful battles, based on inordinate ambitions and self considerations. Let us not forget that we are just trying to recover from the devastating effects of many years of misrule, which has left many of us spiritually depraved, religiously enslaved, socially crippled, culturally disoriented, morally disabled, economically bankrupt, politically distressed, psychologically disturbed, mentally confused, academically paralyzed, intellectually depressed, existentially corrupt and generally insecure. Undoubtedly, we are face with a monumental national disaster which calls for divine intervention.

—Rev. Prof. Yusufu Ameh Obaje.

In the face of unequalled hardships and serious threats to our national survival there is no time left any more to waste on recounting all the negative experiences of our lives, while living in our tribal ghettoes in the land of bondage and captivity. It is equally unredemptive and certainly fruitful at this stage of our national disaster, to use our so-called clever minds or informed active brains simply to engage ourselves in an endless verbal and pen war of apportioning blame on one another, partly to present an ego-centric case designed to make one person or a group of persons solely responsible for turning our God-given semi-paradise into a wasteland of poverty, degradation, violence and untimely deaths. As a matter of urgency, we must forgive one another, join hands together, mobilize ourselves and courageously move forward.

—Rev. Prof. Yusufu Ameh Obaje.

I have a dream that one day we shall become a Nation of God-fearers, with unadulterated faith in one God, which will prompt a spiritual awakening in us, inspire moral consciousness in our daily conduct and cultivate a culture where love for one another, respect for the sacredness of life, justice for all, honesty before God and fellow human-beings, will constitute our life-style...The fear of God should therefore be the beginning of our national deliverance and genuine progress. For, no Nation can develop her national resources to the greater benefit of her citizens, if the people continue to live and behave as if there is no God. I have a dream that one day we shall become a Nation of patriotic and responsible citizens, where unalloyed loyalty to God and to our country Nigeria, shall inform and direct our private and public conduct; where all our God-given resources, talents and potentials shall be devoted to the service of Nigeria in particular and humanity at large; where we shall relentlessly promote the good image of the country, uphold her dignity wherever we are and in whatever we do at any time with all our strength, might and best of our capacity; where we shall give priority attention and commitment to Nigeria as a corporate entity over our inordinate ethnic interest; where we shall selflessly serve and defend Nigeria at all costs and at all times without waiting for personal reward in honour of our corporate existence, survival and progress. We should note that patriotism is an expression of selfless service and commitment to the ideals of one's Nation at all costs and at all times without waiting for personal reward in honour of our corporate existence, survival and progress. We should note that patriotism is an expression of selfless service and commitment to the ideals of one's Nation at all costs and every reasonable situation for the good of the Nation and her entire people. It is different from gratiotism where a gratiot places priority on reward first before any service can be rendered to the Nation.

—Rev. Prof. Yusufu Ameh Obaje.

I have a dream that one day we shall become a Nation of truly reconciled ethnic groups, where we shall live together as real blood brothers and sisters, created in the same and one image of the only true God who is the Lord of all; where we shall love one another, serve one another and celebrate together in times of joy and sorrow; where we shall genuinely relate to one another as fellow citizens, without creating any room or situation for suspicion; where there shall be no more feeling or sense of ethnic domination; where there shall be no more big tribe superiority complex or small tribe inferiority complex; where no one shall feel or act as if Nigeria belongs to his or her own tribe alone; where every Nigerian shall be regarded as a bonafide son or daughter of Nigeria in any part of the country without discrimination, regardless of tribe, religion and status in life.

—Rev. Prof. Yusufu Ameh Obaje.

I have a dream that one day we shall become a Nation of truly liberated people, where no one shall be oppressed; true freedom shall reign in all corners of the country and throughout its length and breadth, height and depth; where everyone shall understand and experience freedom within the cornerstone of community responsibilities—freedom to live a fulfilled life of serving others and to be served by others, while protecting the rights of the community and at the same time safeguarding the privileges of the individual within the community; where our sense of freedom and our appreciation of it shall motivate us to do what is right, and most constructive for the sake of our corporate existence; where no citizen shall be compelled to run away from the country in search of any type of freedom or daily bread; where no one shall yield to the temptation to sell his or her national birthright for a morsel of foreign bread; where no Nigerian shall be under the bondage of satanic forces or cults; where each one shall be free from all avoidable restraints, in order to develop his or her potentials for the benefit of all Nigerians. For as long as citizens of a nation are truly liberated from all unjust structures, systems and destructive powers, they are in a better position to release their best for the progress of the Nation and retain their authentic human existence.

—Rev. Prof. Yusufu Ameh Obaje.

By accident, I was born where I was born…I see myself first as a Nigerian. We should forget that we are either Christians or Muslims, we should forget our ethnicity…

--Gen. Martin Lurther Agwai, rtd.

The prophecy for Nigeria is that we are not in anybody's hands, but in our (Nigerians') hands. Nigeria will change when we sow righteousness, uprightness and integrity, as our expectations shall bring manifestations. Nigerians again should not lose sight of God, hence, all of us should pray fervently against all negative prophecies for the nation

--Prophet Oladipupo Sekunderin.

There are Goliaths, who are spirit in human beings. There are national Goliaths, who bring shame to Nigerians. These people beat their chests to do evil. They don't care about anybody. They are men and women who deny us of electricity, water, good roads, food and so on … There are city Goliaths, community Goliaths, state, regional… There are Goliaths in the arms of government but where are the people of God?

--Pastor Ayo Oritsejafor, CAN President.

I believe in Nigeria, almost in a fanatical manner, because this is a country that has made me who I am today… I therefore always have that strong feeling that I can never sacrifice enough for this great country.

--Prof Dora Akunyili.

We want Nigeria to prosper democratically, politically and socially to provide the basic needs of its people. Our desire for Nigeria is the same desire we have for America.

—Jonnie Carson, American Secretary Of States.

Nigerians have to be resilient and take up the challenge before them; they should never feel defeated or be defeated. Nigerians should never relent. The man that that is a failure is the one who falls and fails to get up. We must keep moving on.

-Mr. Zack Orji, Actor.

As Nigerians home and abroad celebrate the nation.. my message for Nigerians is that they should love one another and pray, not just for themselves, but for the country and leaders.

-Mrs. Aisha Joy.

My message is for God to bless Nigeria. As regards development, we may not have got it right, but God should bless Nigeria and Nigerians. I love Nigeria and I am proud to be a Nigerian. I have no other country.

-Mr. Mdesoji Shiyanbola.

Corruption is the worst form of human rights abuse any one can think of. Corruption is waging war on the rights of the innocent. Corruption is tyrannical; bringing home poverty, deprivation, want, fear and even death to the innocents. Besides, Nigerians are tired of nauseating cries about corruption coming out of quarters strongly suspected to be the haven of corruption. For example, being constantly accused by Nigerians and non-Nigerians the National

Assembly, were the cry about corruption is probably loudest suffers a lot of moral injuries in this regard. We maintain that for the present administration to actualize its lofty promises of transformation agenda to the nation, it must necessarily summon better courage, back speeches with action. This is the only way it can convince Nigerians about its sincerity of purpose.

--Coalition Against Corrupt Leaders.

Beneath the euphoria of self-government, however, lies a gnawing worry: the quality of leaders we have had since independence. It appears the British colonists were kinder to Nigerians than Nigerian leaders have been to their own people. Clearly, this is not the country envisaged by our founding fathers... There is no heinous crime that has not manifested in the country: armed robbery, treasury looting, oil bunkering, 419, political assassinations, ballot thievery, nepotism, bribery and corruption. The moral fibre of our nation has been eaten up by locusts and termites...Many other countries that were on equal standing at independence have since achieved economic independence. Brazil now manufactures aircraft! India, South Korea, North Korea, Indonesia, Malaysia, Singapore—all these countries have positive tales to tell. We cannot claim to be independent when we import nearly everything from all corners of the world...We should start thinking of how to rescue the younger generations from the grip of poverty, ignorance and disease. The fact that millions of Nigerians reside in other countries of the world (legally and illegally) does not speak well of a nation.. The journey to true independence should start from rebuilding our educational institutions and imparting the right education to children who would later grow to be employers, not jobseekers. Nigerian technologists that are in the developed parts of the world should be encouraged to return home to lead our country's industrial revolution. All that is required o achieve these is political will. We urge those who aspire to lead Nigeria .. to reflect deeply on the future of Nigeria and the future generations of Nigerians.

—Leadership Newspaper.

We shall stand up for good governance. We shall defend the interests of the Nigerian state even against its leaders, and we shall raise our pen at all times in defence of what is right. These are the values by which we intend to be assessed.

—Leadership Newspaper.

We have always been a potentially great country. What has been lacking is the kind of leadership that could transform the potential into actuality. We have groped through many thorny paths of fratricidal war. Military rule and democracy, but we are yet to establish institutions that could help to make the nation and its people prosperous. To be sure, we have made some progress. But it hasn't all been a tale of endless woes. Nigerians remain the greatest assets of Nigeria. The people have shown uncommon resilience in the face of unbelievable odds. Our people remain some of the most vibrant and most creative on the planet. In the midst of all the dysfunction around them, Nigerians continue to strive to lift themselves and their country up. The twin evils of terrorism and unbridled corruption stare us in the face. Together, they constitute the most potent threat to the life of the country. There are indications that Boko Haram terrorists have dug in for a prolonged campaign of terror, horror and death. In spite of the gallant efforts of the military, the group continues its campaign of terror, horror and death. In spite of the gallant efforts of the military, the group continues its campaign of cold blooded murders and arson. Beyond making appropriate pronouncements, this is one war the government must bring to a swift and decisive end before it changes the map of Nigeria; terrorists are known to harbor territorial ambition. Indeed, the war against the evils of terrorism and corruption must be won if Nigeria is to survive…we implore everyone to take a hard look at himself or herself. How do we achieve the dreams of our founding fathers? May the labours of our heroes not be in vain.

–Leadership Newspaper.

It is rather unfortunate that 50 years after independence, the office of the presidency of the country is still trivialized along sectional divides. It is a shame that some people were still capitalizing on zoning in a country that claim to be practicing democracy, the presidency of Nigeria is not about North Vs Christians. It is about programme for development, it is about performance or non performance, it is about integrity and accountability. It is about fight against corruption and mismanagement of public funds. And Nigerians, under free and fair election should be allowed to make their choice.

--Leadership Newspaper, June 24, 2010.

Nigeria is not the only multi-ethnic society in the world with diverse cleavages. But unlike other plural societies, including the United States, Canada and India that have forged ahead to create strong and enduring nations from their heterogeneous entities, some Nigerian political leaders think the shortest route to power is to play up those issues that divide the nation. They keep the people apart by latching on to the cleavages for selfish reasons.

--Sunday Punch, May 16, 2010.

The greatest and effective antidote against (disunity) anarchy is effective governance anchored on the principles of fairness, justice and equity, the political class and those in office should place the interest of the nation above parochial consideration.. Our politicians by their disposition appear to have learnt nothing from history.

—Pointer Newspape, Nov 20, 2001.

To make for national development and integration, what is important is how to use presidential power for the greater good of all citizens. It is only when voters are given the right to choose who to govern them, without being inhibited by region, religion, ethnicity and, indeed any harrow-minded consideration, that Nigeria can produce a truly national leader and join the rest of truly democratic world...

--Sunday Punch, May 16, 2010.

One of the basic elements of democracy is equality of all before the law. It is a universal principle and a basic norm that no one is above the law in a democratic polity.

--Nigerian Tribune, July 30, 2001.

Nigeria does not have problems with generation of good ideas. It is effective implementation of policies, and corruption, which derail our good initiatives.

--Daily Sun Newspaper.

This is tragic. They are laying a dangerous precedent for other regions to follow. The way it stands now, there is no guarantee that there will be peace in one zone or region if a man from another zone or region emerges as the President of the country tomorrow. These seeds of discord have been sown and they have germinated and the plants are producing hydra-headed monsters as fruits. This must stop. Fellow citizens, it is also important that we recognize these people for who they are. They are not even qualified to open the front door of hell talk of sermonizing about the civilized conduct in the affairs of men. They mouth preachments to deceive and or confuse the unwary. They were, have been and remain the problem of our country. It is our collective civil and patriotic responsibility to support the government so that it would succeed for our common good not for us to allow space to politicians and their cohorts who are planning to hijack our common patrimony for their personal gains or where that fails create sufficient crisis to foster instability in the polity. We must reject any action based on primordial sentiments and ignore the empty swagger of those who insist they must govern this country at all costs. We are practicing a presidential democracy, so the rules must be followed based on the constitution of the country not intimidation or blackmail. We must remain eternally vigilant in the protection of our collective destiny as a nation and constantly remind ourselves that the whole goal of the destabilization campaign by those who are fanning embers of trouble is to weaken our country internally . . . We must not allow these rouge agents create the platform and set the stage for mutual suspicion among our people so much so that it may lead to the full rapture of the Nigerian stage. Without thinking clearly, as a result of their sponsored bombings, sectarian violence, ethnic leanings and permanent political discord thereby stretching the resources of the government, they may drag us to total catastrophe. We must stand up and fight for the government and for the unity of our country. Fellow compatriots, our country calls. Let us rise and obey. Let us defend our democracy and our nation, the time is now. The urgency of the moment beckons on us.

—Shehu U. Sani etal , Network For National Progress.

APPENDICES

THIS IS NIGERIA, THIS IS WHO WE REALLY ARE

Nigeria is a West African country, the most populous black nation on earth and comes 'number eight' in world's population ranking.
It is a country richly blessed with both human and material resources. Nigerian scientists and other professionals are ranked among the best and ply their trades across the globe.

Nigeria has since time contributed greatly to the development or advancement of this world. Indeed there is hardly any country under the sun that has not felt the positive impact of Nigeria(ns) in his/her developmental process.

Nigeria is indeed a great nation made up of wonderful people. It is the land that produced the legendary "Zik of Africa" and Chinua Achebe (the literary icon). It is good to note that the following people are Nigerians: Prof. Wole Soyinka (the Nobel Laureate), Chimamanda Adichie (a well-celebrated young award-winning author), famed Philip Emeagwali (the father of modern computer and internet, designer of the fastest computer in the world), Ngozi Okonjo-Iweala (MD of World Bank), Jelani Aliyu (the great car designer at General Motors), Damian Anyanwu (an American-based electronic expert), Aliko Dangote (Business mogul and world's twenty fifth richest man), Oby Ezekwesili (former VP World Bank), Ngozi Achebe (Doctor-writer and popular novelist); Prof. Dora Akunyili (the greatest drug war fighter of all times) among such illustrious citizens.Nigeria has countless number of well-known footballers across the world, and even our citizens play in foreign national teams (including U.S.A, Italy, Portugal, etc). Our Nollywood is one of the first three largest film industries in this world.

Nigeria is third world's highest producer of palm oil, she has second highest bitumen deposit in the world, she is ranked sixth world's producer of crude oil, and comes tenth in ranking as regards to gas deposit. And there is hardly any natural mineral that cannot be found beneath Nigeria's soil. In the same vein, Nigeria is the sixteenth world (and Africa's second) highest producer of tomatoes. Surely, no country is as blessed as Nigeria.

Nigeria is a tourist destination, a peaceful country, about 923, 768.48 square Kilometres large: with the expanse space stretching east of Benin Republic, south of Niger and Chad Republics, west of Cameroon and north of the Gulf of Guinea.

Nigeria is, indeed, the wonder of the world: with a population of over one hundred and fifty million people, she is the home of about two hundred and fifty tribes, and close to five hundred dialectical languages. Nigeria is indeed the Giant of Africa, and the pride of the black race!

SOME FACTS ABOUT NIGERIA

Motto: Unity, Faith, Peace and Progress
Location: West Africa, between lat.. ° of Equator and long...°E of Greenwich Meridian
Area: about 923, 768.48 square Kilometres
Current Capital: Abuja (since December 12, 1991)
Population: about 170 million
Number of tribes/Languages: over 250
Major tribes/Languages: Hausa, Yoruba and Igbo
Official languages (Lingua Franca): English
Dialects: Over 500
Major religions: Christainity, Islam, Peganism
Number of Geo-Political Zone: 6
Number of States: 36
Number of L.G.As:774
Number of Senatorial Zones: 109
Number of Federal Constituencies: 360
Number of Electoral Wards:
Biggest state by land-mass: Niger (76, 363 Km^2)
Smallest state by land-mass: Lagos (3, 345 Km^2)
Climate: Tropical
Vegetation: Forest grass-land and semi-arid
Time Zone: GMT + 1 hour
Currency: Naira and Kobo
Chief foreign exchange/income earner: petroleum

NATIONAL CURRENCIES AND SYMBOLS

Nigeria flag: with colour of **Green-White-Green**

National Coat Of Arms: **with two horses and a perching eagle**

N5 note has the portrait of Sir Tafawa Balewa(1st and only Prime Minister of Nigeria)

N10 note has the portrait of Alvan Ikoku (Educationist).

N20 note has the portrait of Gen. Murtala Mohammed.

N50 note has pictorial representations of three ethnic groups WAZOBIA

N100 note has the portrait of Obafemi Awolowo (1st Premier of Western Nigeria).

N200 note has the portrait of Ahmadu Bello (1st and only Premier of Northern Nigeria).

N500 note has the portrait of Nnamdi Azikiwe (1st and only Governor General of Nigeria

RELIGIOUS HOLIDAYS/NATIONAL DAYS IN NIGERIA

Armed Forces Remembranceday: January 15

May/Workers' Day: May 1

Democracy Day: May 29

Children's Day: May 27

Democracy Day: May 29

Independence Day: October 1

Big Hajj Day:

Small Hajj Day:

Easter Day:

Christmas Day: December 25

Boxing Day: December 25

PARTING WORDS

".the society is ours, if we do not say, who will say, if we do not act who will act?"

– Chairman Mao Zedong (former Chinese Leader).

Criticism more than familiar rituals of adulation is a higher form of patriotism.

-Albert   Camus.

There is nothing as important in any nation as peace

—Nelson Mandela.

BOOKS BY THE AUTHOR

1. You Can Still Succeed And Even Lead
2. Why Wondering And Wandering
3. Let Not Your Heart Be Dismayed
4. Inspire Your World In Times Like This
5. It Will Be Better If You Will Not Surrender
6. No Cause For Alarm
7. Trials Are Temporal
8. More Than A Conqueror
9. Success Is Just A Step Further
10. Meditating On His Goodness And Mercy
11. In God I Wholly Trust
12. You Can Reach The Top If You Refuse To Stop
13. Understanding This Life
14. Anyone Can Be A Star Who Dares To Start
15. Break The Barrier And Net The Goal
16. Discover And Recover In Times Like This
17. The Task To Make Nigeria Great Is A Task For Everyone
18. Echoes Of Trillion Woes And Zillion Foes
19. Lachrymal Lines Of A Lonely Voice
20. This Thing Called Love
21. A Story Told By An Idiot
22. Immortal Lines
23. Trillion Ants In Pants
24. Join In The Effort To Remake Nigeria
25. Let Us Think And Talk Nigeria First
26. Learnfast Mathematics
27. Teachme Mathematics
28. New Scholarship Mathematics
29. Mastering Physics Formulas
30. Calculations In Physics